The Physician Philosopher's Guide to Personal Finance:

The 20% of Personal Finance Doctors Need to Know to Get 80% of the Results

By: James D. Turner, MD
The Physician Philosopher, LLC

Foreword by James M. Dahle, MD
Founder of The White Coat Investor

Editor: Kim Watkins
Cover by: Praveen at fluto.design

AISN: B07N54T4ZY (Ebook)
ISBN-13: 978-0-578-44870-1: (paperback)

For more information, please visit:
ThePhysicianPhilosopher.com

First Edition
Printed in the United States of America

Disclosure: The views expressed within this book are the views of the author alone. They do not reflect the views of the author's employer, Wake Forest Baptist Medical Center. As such the author's employer should not be held liable or responsible for any views expressed within this book.

Dedicated to all medical students, residents, and fellows. It is a privilege to teach you; may we never forget that.

Keep up the good work

Adam!

Acknowledgements

Writing The Physician Philosopher's Guide to Personal Finance took the better part of a year, and it involved the help of several people. First, and foremost, I need to thank my wife and our three little philosophers for allowing me the time to write. While I mostly wrote during naps and night time when the kids were asleep, it was time spent looking at a computer screen instead of spending time with my family. Kristen, I am thankful that you support my passions, and I am even more thankful that God let me marry the best person that I know. You are an amazing wife and mother, and I am honored to be your "lesser half".

After writing the book, I sent the first (very rough) copy to one of my best friends, Michael Kittner. His knowledge of personal finance is part of what sparked my original interest. For that, and Mike's friendship, I'll always be thankful. I wouldn't have given anyone else a first crack. And, it didn't hurt that Mike is married to one of the best doctors I know.

Other people who were kind enough to review later editions of the book included a college friend of mine who is also a fellow physician, Lee Day MD; Dr. McFrugal (of drmcfrugal.com); Justin Serette, MD; Zachary McKee MD; Andrew Reaven MD; and David Lifferth MD.

A big thanks also goes to one of our best friends, and the editor of this book, Kim Watkins. Her editorial work really turned this book into a much more professional endeavor. I don't deserve the pedigree of editorial help that she provided, but I am eternally thankful for her help (and friendship) nonetheless.

I also need to thank those that have gone before me in trailblazing this path. This includes James M. Dahle, MD - the White Coat Investor - who was kind enough to write a foreword for this book; and Physician on Fire who has been second to none in helping me out from the beginning.

Thank you also to those that were involved in the creation of the cover of this book. Who knew that a cover contest could produce such a good result! Specifically, I'd like to thank Praveen of fluto.design (https://fluto.design/for-authors.html).

Thanks also to The Physician Philosopher email subscribers who were willing to comment and vote in the book cover design contest.

Jimmy
~The Physician Philosopher

Table of Contents

Foreword

This is a $2 Million book. As I have canvassed the country, both online and in person over the last 8 years, I have frequently told physicians and dentists that the first really good personal finance and investing book you ever read is likely to be worth $2 Million to you over the course of your life. This book certainly qualifies. Financial books are never going to be as entertaining as Harry Potter, but if the next four hours with this book are likely to be worth $2 Million to you, I am sure you would agree it would be worth a little time and effort to earn $500,000 an hour.

In my experience, the reputation doctors have for poor financial decisions is well-deserved, although we have been on a steep learning curve these last few years thanks to people like Dr. James D. Turner, the author of this book. Bad decisions and misaligned priorities add up quickly when combined with a physician income. When you add in the cost of even an average-priced financial advisor, literally millions of dollars have disappeared by the end of a career. That money could have been used to pay off student loans faster, pay off mortgages, provide retirement security, help our children avoid the same kinds of educational debt we faced, and support our favorite charitable causes. Instead, the money was primarily transferred out of physician's pockets and into that of the financial services industry.

In some ways doctors are like athletes, artists, and performers. We make a high income based on some well-honed knowledge or talent we have that is not related to running a business. By the time business owners reach a physician-like income, they have learned many lessons in the school of hard knocks. They have learned to negotiate. They have learned to recognize a good deal and a bad deal. They have learned to be careful about debt, to analyze a balance sheet and an income sheet, and to live on a careful budget. They know that those in the business world are primarily looking out for number one, not a patient they have sworn to serve. While ethics certainly matter in the business world (who is going to do business twice with a crook?) there is no Hippocratic Oath administered at the end of business school. Meanwhile, the doctor enters the real world in her mid-30s already with a high income (although typically with a negative net worth) but without having learned any of those same lessons. This is a recipe for financial disaster.

In The Physician Philosopher's Guide to Personal Finance, Dr. Turner has done a marvelous job of compiling the critical financial lessons that were never taught to you in school, residency, or fellowship. The most important of these is found in the title of Chapter Nine, just four simple words – Live Like A Resident. It is so simple, although not easy given the immense pressure to spend that doctors face from patients, society, family, friends, and frankly their own expectations. Yet this is actually the secret to wealth as a physician. Those who do it nearly always become wealthy and those who do not typically have a difficult time reaching even reasonable financial goals. In recent years, as the cost of education has skyrocketed without an accompanying increase in physician incomes, living like a resident for a few years after training has become even more critical.

Living like a resident means that when you leave your training and your income quadruples or quintuples, that you maintain a lifestyle similar to what you enjoyed on your trainee income. You then use the difference between your attending income and your resident-level expenditures to build wealth. If that seems a bit difficult after all those years of delayed gratification, give yourself a small raise. In fact, give yourself a HUGE raise—maybe even a 50% raise. In corporate America, that sort of a raise is almost unheard of. But if it allows you to avoid the lifestyle explosion of the typical graduating resident (often the equivalent of a 300-400% raise), it will be worth it. The "Live Like A Resident" period should last 2-5 years after training. This will allow you to pay off all of your student loans, save up a down payment on your dream house, and catch up to your college roommates (who have probably already been making good money for a decade by now) with regards to retirement savings. You will be able to enjoy that fancy doctor car, that fancy doctor house, and those fancy doctor vacations eventually. But you need to take care of business first. What are two more years when you have 30-40 more in your career and perhaps 60-70 left on the planet?

Physician burnout and suicide is at epidemic levels. While solid financial management certainly does not solve all problems, it is hard to get burned out at a job you can walk away from at any time. Having your financial ducks in a row provides a sense of hope at those times when you feel that you are repeatedly slamming your head into a keyboard while fighting what appears to be the world's worst electronic medical record. I am convinced that good financial planning reduces physician stress, burnout, suicide, and divorce. Rather than making the rich richer, this work is healing the healers. A doctor who does not need her next paycheck, with enough money in the bank, can make decisions that prolong her career, promote her wellness, and provide better patient care rather than succumbing to the pressures of an increasingly profit-centered health care system. While I cannot prove it with a double-blind, placebo-controlled study, I am convinced that teaching doctors the basic principles of personal finance and investing actually improves patient care. Yes, a few people will apply those principles to allow themselves an early retirement from medicine. The truth is we do not want those folks practicing medicine anyway. If you are a patient, you want someone taking care of you that would do so whether their net worth was -$200,000 or $10 Million. We do not want our doctors to feel trapped in the medical rat race due to their massive student loan burdens, mortgages, and lifestyle. That is not good for anyone.

My favorite part of this book is the application of the Pareto Principle to your personal finances—20% of the effort produces 80% of the results. This applies to finance just as much as it does to medicine and anything else. While there is a lifetime of learning waiting for you, it really does not take that long to understand the high yield material. The financial world has its own language, but once you learn it you will realize this stuff is far easier than nephrology, otorhinolaryngology, or the underrated task of sifting through hundreds of the worried well in search of the well-appearing but deathly ill. You do not have to know everything to manage your own money well and thanks to the appearance of low-priced, competent financial planners and investment managers on the scene, you do not even have to do it all on your own to be successful.

I was pleased to see Dr. Turner dedicate two full chapters in this book to the management of student loans. For the young attending or trainee, this is the elephant in the room of their personal finances. In fact, managing and eliminating student loans is really the practice run for building your retirement nest egg. If you drag those loans out for decades, you will likely never build the kind of wealth you will need to support a comfortable retirement lifestyle. Take them in the corner and drop an anvil on them. That will give you the skills, knowledge, confidence, and frankly the "financial muscles" you need to then build a seven figure nest egg—what Jonathan Clements has referred to as the "greatest financial task of our lives."

In reality, financial planning is not just about money. Money is really just a store of life-energy—a combination of our time and work—since that is what we exchanged for it. The goal is not to acquire more money than the next person. The goal is to spend your life energy in a way that is likely to maximize your happiness and that of others you care about. We save and invest in order to spend and give more later than we could today. You want to earn, save, invest, spend, and give intentionally and intelligently to maximize that happiness. In fact, a typical physician in many ways has resources that are more unlimited than those of the planet. If everyone on the planet consumed in the way that a doctor can afford to, it would likely cause environmental catastrophes the human race could not survive. Thus, frugality is not just a financial skill, but also an environmental movement.

You have dedicated your life to the healing of the sick and injured. Thank you for doing that. I know you go many days sometimes without a single patient showing you gratitude for your sacrifices. In this book, Dr. Turner will be serving you just like you serve your patients. Take advantage of his efforts and experience. By doing so, you will benefit your family, your patients, and yourself.

James M. Dahle, MD
Founder of The White Coat Investor

Chapter 1: Introduction

If you can talk with crowds and keep your virtue,
Or walk with Kings—nor lose the common touch,
If neither foes nor loving friends can hurt you,
If all men count with you, but none too much;
If you can fill the unforgiving minute
With sixty seconds' worth of distance run,
Yours is the Earth and everything that's in it,
And—which is more—you'll be a Man, my son!
~ Rudyard Kipling, "If"

Reading this book will be like climbing a mountain.

You are the climber taking your first trek up the steep side of a mountain called "Mount Retirement." You will be led by me, a common journeyman who has become a Sherpa, or guide. My job is to come down the mountain, guide you back up, and warn you of potential pitfalls and failures along the way. When you reach the top of the precipice, you will understand that this seemingly complicated topic is actually pretty easy to understand—you just need to know where to locate the footholds.

I've made plenty of mistakes along the way and have witnessed countless other mistakes friends and colleagues have made. Most of these mistakes occurred because no one warned us. My goal is to help you avoid these errant paths and to set you up for financial success with a "set it and forget it" method.

This book is specifically written for medical students, residents, and early career physicians with hopes of making you aware of the financial goals you should be striving to achieve—and then to show you how to achieve them. If you are a high-income earner or in a medical profession of a different variety, this book will likely be helpful for you, too.

What will you learn in this book?

I will cover a lot of topics in this book in a relatively brief amount of time. Trust me, I know how busy you are and I am not trying to make your life any busier!

Here are some of the essential topics:
- Investing basics (compound interest, time in the market versus "timing" the market, etc.)
- Investing specifics (types of vehicles, solid investment plans, and examples)
- Specifics on how to attack your student loans
- Paying off debt versus investing (or both) at various stages
- Asset protection (life, disability, umbrella insurance, etc.)
- Where to get financial advice and identifying where conflicts of interest exist
- Why lifestyle inflation matters after training and how it can wreck your life

Ultimately, this book is a "how-to guide" on achieving financial success *without* having to learn all of the intricacies. You will be able to do it all yourself. If that sounds daunting, just let me take you on a little ride. If by the end of it all you still feel overwhelmed, then by all means give me a shout and I'll be happy to help point you in the right direction.

What is my personal finance philosophy?

My interest in personal finance and debt management came pretty late in my training after I had already completed my anesthesiology residency. In fact, my interest started when I was in my fellowship in regional anesthesia. I started having conversations with various people and realized rather quickly there was a big knowledge gap when it came to personal finance topics. This led me to start a website, The Physician Philosopher (thephysicianphilosopher.com), where I write about these things to help the medical community obtain wealth without forgotting why we build wealth in the first place—to live an intentional and balanced life.

In a nutshell, I want you to get to financial independence as quickly and as easily as possible, while still enjoying the ride. I use an evidence-based "set it and (mostly) forget it" investing model to help you get there. You have enough on your hands taking care of patients. My goal is to make this as simple as it can be and only as complicated as it must be. By learning the basics that this book provides, you will beat the vast majority of investors. That's not because I'm going to provide you a magic bullet, but because you will understand that keeping it simple wins.

My world view on personal finances is about accomplishing a balance between obtaining financial independence as early as possible, but I still want you to enjoy today. As medical professionals, we are all too aware of our mortality. Today, or any day, could be our last. For this reason, I do not want you to miss out on the here and now. My plan allows you to be reasonable about accomplishing this balance.

Why should you read this book?

What if someone told you that you could finish training, practice medicine for 10 to 15 years, and then—if you follow the steps outlined in this book—choose to practice medicine because you *want* to and not because you *have* to? That sounds pretty good, doesn't it?

That, my friends, is called financial independence. Financial independence is the point at which you no longer need to work to earn a paycheck because your savings, investments, and/or passive income streams can now support you exclusively. You could also retire early at this point, but my aim is not to deplete this country of its doctors. My aim is to help you achieve financial freedom so that you get to practice medicine how you want and as much (or as little) as you want.

I still haven't answered the question of *why* you should read this book, though. The real reason is that we have a physician wellness problem in our country. In fact, the 2018 Medscape National Physician Burnout and Depression Report showed that 42% of physicians are burned out[1]. When you combine burnout with financial stress, work-life stress, and regular everyday stress,

―――――――――――――

[1] Medscape. Medscape National Physician Burnout & Depression Report 2018. https://www.medscape.com/slideshow/2018-lifestyle-burnout-depression-6009235#2. Accessed January 15, 2019.

you get a recipe for disaster. This book will empower you to take hold of your finances so that you can live the life you want to live. Financial independence will help you combat the ever-present threat of burnout. Financial independence will allow you to work full-time (or part-time) without having the real threat of losing your autonomy to administrators and bureaucrats. Financial independence also provides the power you need to break free of the shackles of debt that intend to ensnare you.

Why do I want to help you?

There are a lot of reasons to help, but here is the biggest: Doctors love helping people. It's really that simple.

I chose to become an academic anesthesiologist. I stayed in academics after finishing my own training because I love teaching students, residents, and fellows. Helping and teaching people are my two passions in life. When I do that well and people find it helpful, I feel fulfilled. What I am saying is that you should read this book because it helps me feel satisfied in life.

All kidding aside, I wrote this book because it is the one I would have liked to have read as a trainee. It would have saved me a lot of trouble and money. It would have allowed me to pay off my debt sooner and get to financial independence faster. I didn't know forbearance and deferment were terrible ideas. So, I signed up. I didn't know the difference between stocks and bonds or actively managed mutual funds and passive/index funds. A Backdoor Roth IRA? What's that? You mean the government will pay some of my interest each month if enrolled in certain income-driven repayment programs? How should I have known to wait until residency to apply for disability insurance with my medical history?

Even if you are a financial wizard, this book contains helpful information that you will find interesting. Financial topics can be profoundly complicated. They don't have to be, though, and this book will teach you the necessary information for success.

How will I teach this to you?

I won the Golden Apple Award—given to the best teacher in the department as voted on by the residents—in my first year as an attending physician. Some say that I won because I paid the residents to vote for me. I don't blame them for thinking that. No one had ever won the Golden Apple in their first year. The truth is much more interesting; I simply pulled the wool over their eyes!

See, I am a simple man who needs concepts to be as simple as possible in order for me to understand. Complicated stuff makes my head spin. I'm not smart enough to keep up with it. The best teachers make complicated concepts easy to understand, so you can see why the residents were confused. My goal in this book is to fool you in the same way I fooled my residents by making a complicated topic like physician finance digestible. This will happen using the **Pareto Principle**, which holds that 20% of the work accomplishes 80% of the intended results. What exactly does that mean? An analogy may be helpful here.

Navigating personal finance and debt management is just like driving a car. Cars can be complicated, if you want them to be. If you wanted to understand everything there is to know about cars, you would need a keen understanding of fluid hydraulics, friction, gear ratios, piston mechanics, and how to appropriately wire the sound system. It's certainly possible to learn all of this. There are books on automobile mechanics and physics, not to mention schools that you could attend for a complete education.

I am willing to bet, though, that when you get into your car these areas of expertise do not cross your mind. All that most people really want is to understand the 20% about cars that help them accomplish a car's purpose: getting from point A to point B safely and in comfort. The 20% of driving a car that you need involves turning an ignition, using the accelerator (I can't use "gas pedal" anymore now that we have electric cars), pressing the brakes, turning the steering wheel, controlling the electrical instruments in the car, and knowing how often the car needs maintenance. You could learn everything else there is to know, but it wouldn't help you get from A to B more safely or in more comfort.

Personal finance is the exact same way. We can make it as complicated as our hearts desire. We could dive into safe withdrawal rates and discuss the Trinity Study, sequence of return risks, the efficient frontier, tax-loss harvesting, pre-tax versus Roth investing, algorithm-based investing, or investing with a tilt towards small and value-based factors. And we will discuss some of that. However, it will only be what you need to know.

The truth of the matter is that you need to know 20% of personal finance and debt management to get 80% of the results. All we want is to get from point A (being a broke medical student/resident/physician) to point B (financial independence). The trouble is in knowing which 20% is the important 20%. That's what this book will teach you.

Disclosure

I need to disclose some information. I do not hold any degrees in finance. I am not a financial advisor, attorney, or accountant. What I am is a physician who has walked in your shoes, knows your plight, and can relate to your current situation. My expertise is in the field of medicine; specifically in anesthesiology and regional anesthesia. So, all of the information in this book comes from the perspective of a physician who got hoodwinked enough times to start learning this stuff on his own and to write a book so that it wouldn't happen to you. It is a book written for your general education, and you should verify anything you learn with a reputable source. Take that for what it's worth.

If you want to hear more from me, I encourage you to visit and subscribe to my website: The Physician Philosopher (thephysicianphilosopher.com/subscribe). Sign up to see the posts that I create each week, which are targeted at medical students, residents, and early career medical professionals.

Chapter 2: Personal Finance Basics

*"Compound interest is the eighth wonder of the world.
He who understands it, earns it ... he who doesn't ...
pays it.
Compound interest is the most powerful force in the
universe."*
~ Einstein (Debated)

I have a few pet peeves in the teaching world. One of the biggest is when people use medical slang or acronyms in front of medical trainees. This bothers me because medical trainees are in a place of subordination. They are learners. If someone uses a word that they don't understand, they will usually nod along with the conversation, as if they understand everything, rather than risk the embarrassment of admitting they don't know something to the people who will be grading their performance. They often fail to speak up out of fear of a bad evaluation or retribution, at the expense of their education.

An example from the world of anesthesiology is when a patient's oxygen saturation declines quickly after the induction of anesthesia. My residents often say things like, *"Man, this guy's 'sat' just tanked. He doesn't have any 'reserve'!"* When working with me, the person talking like this gets to answer some fun questions, particularly if they made the comment in front of students. *"What exactly is a 'sat'? How does it work? What do you mean by 'reserve'? Explain that to me."*

If I don't ask those questions, I risk assuming that the learners in the room understand the physiological principles of oxygen consumption, light wavelength frequencies of oxygenated and deoxygenated blood, and functional residual capacity, which are critical to understanding anesthesiology.   Frankly, without understanding these concepts, you cannot do my job. For this reason—and because I was a philosophy major in college—clean definitions are critical while learning something new.

Personal finance topics are no different. It is important to make clear definitions and to define the learner's knowledge gap.   After this has been determined, the gap can be filled intentionally and completely.

Defining and Filling the Gap

In academic medicine, the attending physician needs to accomplish two main objectives when it comes to educating trainees:
1) Find the learner's knowledge gaps.
2) Fill in those knowledge gaps.

Because this is a book, asking questions and getting answers proves problematic. Finding your knowledge gaps would be difficult without harnessing the powers of ESP (extrasensory perception for the non-science fiction geeks).   So, this book won't make any assumptions about what you do and don't know. Readers who already know this introductory stuff, stick with me for a chapter or two. Or just skip ahead, you *know-it-alls*. I don't mind. In fact, I won't even know— unless I have ESP!

Let's discuss earning capacity versus investing capital. We will then turn to compound interest, building wealth, and budgeting (yes, I just said the "B" word).

Earning Capacity Versus Investing Capital

For most doctors, the lowest point in their net worth journey is right when they finish training. My net worth was negative $208,000 at that time. Most early career attending physicians have high debt from student loans and consumer or credit cards and low investments totals. It probably hasn't crossed your mind, but at this point in your career a newborn infant without a penny to her name is worth more than you. Your net worth is likely *negative*.

Fortunately, you have one thing in your favor right when finishing training: your earning capacity. Some people also refer to this as "human capital." The point is this: When you are young, your earning capacity is large because you have many years ahead where you will have a very high income earning potential.

However, your investing capital is quite low, because most people haven't started investing heavily at this stage. Your savings rate determines returns for a long time before interest ever really matters. Most have very little saved when they finish, which means that interest is actively working against them while they carry debt. Fortunately for the young physician, this can be overcome because your earning capacity is quite high! They are set to earn millions of dollars over the next 20 to 30 years.

All of this is for naught, though, if they don't use that high earning capacity to save money and build wealth. If they spend it all on lifestyle inflation for their current self (houses, cars, private school, etc.), they leave very little for their future self. No one likes dying poor, but most people say *"I'll just get to it later, I've got lots of time."*

Recognize that your earning capacity is large when you are young. Use this to have a high savings rate. That way, compound interest will become your friend, and not your foe. An additional point to be made early and often is that *wealth* is not the same thing as *income*.

Compound Interest (Friend or Foe?)

Whether Einstein actually said the quote at the beginning of this chapter is irrelevant (though it is often debated). The truth of the quote is evident, if you understand compound interest. Let's use an example.

If you have $1,000,000 in the stock market and your investments grow by 10% interest, you will earn $100,000 *a year* simply having that money sitting in the market. If you have $3,000,000 in the same market, you would earn $300,000 a year. This is passive income—you do no active work to make money. It is one of the many ways the "rich get richer." Money can work for you once you gain enough momentum. Compound interest can be your friend.

However, it must be said that compound interest is often not your friend at the end of training. One could argue that for the roughly 80% of the medical students who finish training with student loan debt, compound interest is actually an active foe. If your student loans are compounded annually and you are being charged 7% interest on those loans, the pain will be very real. If you have $200,000 in student loan debt (the national average) at 7% interest rate, compound interest will increase your debt by $14,000 a year. Go into forbearance and let that compound over the course of a five-year residency. You no longer owe $200,000; you now owe around $280,000. That's a big difference.

So, the goal with compound interest is to make it work *for* you and not *against* you. The eventual goal is to make sure you have lots of assets invested in the market and no debt. Being debt-free means that compound interest can only work *for* you.

The Rule of 72

Any conversation involving compound interest would be incomplete without introducing The Rule of 72. The first person to introduce this to me was Physician on Fire. The rule is simple. To determine how long it will take for money to double, divide 72 by the interest rate. For example, if money is compounding at 8% interest then you can expect the money to double in 9 years (72 / 8 = 9).

The rule of 72 teaches us a few things:
1) The higher the compound interest you are earning in the market, the faster your money will double.
2) The longer you stay in the market, the more time your money has to double (or triple or quadruple).

3) You should aim for investments that will consistently get you the highest returns with the least risk. In other words, efficient investing is the goal.

Building Wealth

In this discussion on financial success and financial independence, we must continue our conversation with clear definitions. We said earlier that financial independence is the point at which you no longer have to keep working. In other words, you have built enough wealth—or have enough passive income—that you no longer need to keep building.

Wealth is often measured by something called "net worth." Simply put, net worth = assets - debts. It follows that the more assets and the less debt you have, the more wealth you possess. Notice that equation says nothing about your income. While income and wealth are related, they are distinctly different.

Here is another confusing premise for many: spending loads of money does not equate with being wealthy. Buying the doctor car or the doctor house may make you look wealthy, but usually these purchases send people deeper into debt. If you have been paying attention, more debt = less wealthy. This sounds pretty simplistic, but it is an often misunderstood concept. How many times growing up or in training have you seen the attending physician who drives the BMW, Audi, or Alfa Romeo? What about the doctor house? You know, the one you walk into and say, "*Wow, this is really nice … I can't wait to have this someday.*" They look like they are living the good life.

What those people are living is likely not the "good life" at all. They are more likely living the "in debt" life. It is a shackle that binds them fast. Spending money does *not* make a person wealthy. It often means the exact opposite. The less debt people have the more likely that it is they are wealthy. The flip side is also true. The more debt they have, the less likely they are to be wealthy.

Don't get caught in the trappings of pretend wealth. When you see others spending money that they probably don't have, don't covet their possessions. The appropriate emotion is pity: you should feel bad for them. Instead of being jealous, why not just buy them a book on eliminating debt while you enjoy your early financial independence that you'll learn about in this book and on my site, The Physician Philosopher (thephysicianphilosopher.com/about)

Budgeting

If our goal is to obtain early financial independence through building wealth by investing aggressively in assets and destroying our debt, then we need to have a keen idea of where our money is going. Simply put, you can't put money towards assets or debts if you don't have any idea where your money is going. The tool required here is a budget.

Unfortunately, the word "budget" has garnered negative press lately. If you prefer to think of this as "tracking spending" that is fine. The point is that the people who are successful with their money have a very good idea of how much money they are bringing in, how much they are spending, and precisely where their money is going. Budgeting should occur on a monthly basis for three to six months. After the first few months, look through your budget and then make intentional decisions about what is worth spending money on and what needs to be cut.

For my medical student and resident friends, I recognize your income is limited. After you have made sense of your finances, you will have a good idea of how much money you can afford to put towards building wealth. Early in training, your money should be spent on minimizing debt. As a resident, your choice between investing or paying down debt is more complicated (see chapter 8). Either way, learn to be intentional with money and to prepare for future expenses, such as residency or fellowship interviews, by saving and budgeting for them

For my graduating residents/fellows and early career attending physicians, the above lessons need to be taken to heart. To succeed, you must pay yourself before you budget. Specific tips and tricks will be discussed in the chapter on investing after residency, but while we are discussing budgets it should be pointed out that your budget should not include money going towards investments. Before you figure your budget, pay your student loans, 401K/403B, backdoor Roth, taxable account, and other investment vehicles such as a 529. Consider these as non-negotiable and outside of your budget. The remaining money is the starting point for your budget. This is sometimes called "paying yourself first" (or last, depending on how you think about it).

There are many tools out there that can help you track your spending. Some of my favorites include Mint, You Need a Budget, and Personal Capital. However, there is nothing wrong with using your bank account and a plain old excel spreadsheet with your spending categories. Just do something you can stick with that will help you make intentional decisions about your spending.

An Emergency Fund

We are putting the cart before the horse a little bit here. Before we discuss the purpose and reason behind making a financial plan, most financial experts would recommend having a small amount of asset protection in place. This is often called an emergency fund, and it's really important to have, particularly early in your career. The purpose of an emergency fund is to have enough money in an easily accessible account to afford unexpected expenses that arise from a minor or major calamity.

The real reason for an emergency fund is to prevent you from making a financially catastrophic mistake, such as dipping into your retirement accounts or going further into debt, if you lose your source of income or have a major unexpected expense. Examples that may require large payments could include the gap before long-term disability payments would kick in should you become disabled, a large unexpected health care bill, a house fire, or a job loss. The emergency fund ensures enough cash is immediately available that you could easily pay for any of these things without stealing from a retirement account.

Your emergency funds can be placed in a money market account, regular savings account, checking account, or taxable account invested in very low-risk investments. For my medical student friends, this might involve minimizing student loan withdrawals and having any unclaimed loans serve as a backup, if needed.

Dave Ramsey, an expert on destroying debt, recommends $1,000 for an initial emergency fund. He recommends building up to a 3-6 month supply for a larger emergency fund. A fund of between $1,000 and $2,000 is pretty reasonable as a resident. So long as the deductibles on most insurance products are not more than this amount, $1,000-$2,000 should cover most unexpected expenses. While credit cards do have a place and a purpose, in my opinion they are not to be used as an emergency fund. Simply have the cash available to pay. If the emergency fund is depleted because of an unexpected cost, fill it back up before working on other goals, such as paying down debt or investing again.

Once you become an attending physician, it is usually advisable to have 3 to 6 months of living expenses saved. Many disability insurance policies kick in after 6 months of disability. For this reason alone, you need to be able to bridge that gap should you need it.

Make a Financial Plan

Another quote with debatable authorship is often attributed to Benjamin Franklin:

"If you fail to plan, you plan to fail."

There's a lot to learn from this quote, and it directly relates to what is being discussed in this chapter. The information above is all well and good, but if you don't have a plan it will all fall through. Life is about making intentional decisions and sticking to them.

For example, you might have a tough time getting into medical school if you knew nothing about the GPA that was required, especially if you spent most of your time in college playing beer pong or pick-up basketball instead of studying. What if you didn't realize there were resources to study for the MCAT, and just decided to show up and take the test? That wouldn't go very well, either. What if you didn't know that there was an expectation to wear a suit for medical school interviews, and instead showed up in a Hawaiian shirt? They'd probably tell you *"no, thanks"* at the door.

Of course, this is different than knowing all of the necessary things and not staying committed to the course. I took the MCAT twice, because it didn't go as well as I hoped the first time. The second time I improved by a standard deviation, because I not only knew the plan, but had the fortitude to stick to it. Knowing what to do is half the battle; staying the course provides the remainder of what is required.

In physician finance, the first step is to make some very intentional decisions by creating a financial plan. There are lots of ways to accomplish this. One option is to pay a fee-only advisor (more on that in the next chapter) a few thousand dollars to make a financial plan. Another option is to take the course made by The White Coat Investor.[2]

However you go about making a financial plan, be sure to include specific goals. Give a date by which you hope to achieve each goal. If it's a financial goal, put a number on it. That way, it will be easier to perform the second half of a financial plan: sticking with it. When I finished training, my main goals consisted of having $200,000 in student loans paid off in two years and to have $100,000 in assets in one year. Completing these tasks provided great motivation! Achieving the goals we set encourages us to keep pursuing the other goals on our list.

Aspects of a financial plan

Remember, we are following the Pareto principle. This is the 20% that you need to get 80% of the results. One of the more important reasons to make a plan is that when times get tough, it will be easy to look back and stick to the plan! It's a gentle reminder of where you are going and how you plan to get there.

One word of caution first: Don't let this process intimidate you! By the end of this book, you'll be able to answer all of these questions. Let this list encourage you—you are about to learn everything on it.

Here are the salient aspects of a financial plan:

---

[2] You can check out my review of the Fire Your Financial Advisor course at the following link: (https://thephysicianphilosopher.com/2018/01/26/fire-financial-advisor-review/).

1. **Debt**:
    a. List all of your debts and the dates by which you expect to pay them off. State your specific plan to pay off each item (e.g., I'll pay $5,000 in monthly student loan payments and use additional bonus money to pay off my $200,000 in 24 months).
    b. Do you plan to pursue public service loan forgiveness (PSLF)? If you pursue PSLF, what program(s) will you use to do this? Will you privately refinance your loans? At what point and how? Once your loans are paid off, what will you do with the extra money that you can now cash flow each month? (Hint: You should enjoy some of it and save most of it.)
2. **Spending**:
    a. Timeline: How long will you live like a resident after residency? To what end? How much "lifestyle creep" will you let yourself have after training?
    b. House: When will you buy the doctor house? Will you buy the doctor house at all? How much will you spend? What goals MUST you achieve before you buy a house (debt free, student loans gone, a certain net worth, or after a certain down payment is saved)? How much money will you put down on the house?
    c. Cars: Will you buy used or new cars? How often will you buy them? What criteria must be met before you can

purchase another car (e.g., a 10-year timeline or ability to pay in cash?)?

3. **Saving/Investing**:

a. Emergency fund: How much will you keep in your emergency fund (3-6 months)? Where will you keep it (money market account, bank account, taxable account, etc.)? If you dip into your emergency fund, will you prioritize rebuilding the fund?

b. Retirement: How much will you need to retire? How will you achieve this? By what date? What investment vehicles (403B, 457, Roth IRA, etc.) will you use and in what order will you fund them? What kind of funds will you use to get there (individual stocks, passive or active funds, cryptocurrency)?

c. Net worth goals: What age will you be when you save your first $100,000, $500,000, $1 million, and reach your retirement goal? How will you celebrate each milestone?

d. Investing specifics: If you have consumer and student loan debt, when will you start investing? What asset allocation do you want to keep and for how long? How often will you rebalance and under what conditions? What percentage of your investment accounts do you plan to use each year in retirement? If you plan to retire early, how will you bridge the gap until you can access your retirement accounts?

e. College education: If you have kids, will you help them pay for college? How much will you pay (all, some, none)? How much money will you provide for each kid? By what date do you anticipate having that money?

4. **Sticking to the plan**

   a. Under what circumstances will you sell your assets? Hint: The answer is *not* when the market is down; that's a financial catastrophe when you realize losses by selling low.

   b. How often will you check your portfolio (once a month, once a quarter, once a year, only when you rebalance)? Hint: The less often you look, the more likely you are to leave it alone.

   c. Under what circumstances is it okay to change the plan (mutual agreement between spouse/partner after 3, 6, 9 months)?

Take Home

While preparing a financial plan may seem overwhelming, remember that reading this book is like learning to drive a car. It's not necessary to know everything about friction and the fluid dynamics of car tires on a wet road. That's a part of the 80% that isn't necessary *for you* to know. However, it is necessary to know how to determine if tires are down to the tread wear bar so that the tires can be replaced. That's part of the 20% about tires that you need to get 80% of the results.

When you complete this book, you will know the necessary 20% of physician finance. You need an answer to every single one of the questions above to have a successful financial plan. Don't be distressed! You can do it all yourself. And for the very small portion of you that still can't (or don't want to) do it yourself, you will learn the appropriate resources for questions you cannot answer.

As a recap:
- Make compound interest your friend (not your foe).
- Building wealth means increasing assets and destroying (and preventing the accumulation of) debt.
- Learn to budget or track spending.
- Start an emergency fund.
- After all the numbers are clear from the budget, make a very specific and achievable plan with target dates set for each goal.
- Stick to the plan.

It is also prudent to mention that you should maintain your financial bearings once you complete your initial education. Consider following one of the many physician finance blogs that exist. I have a list of recommended physician finance websites.[3] If you would like to sign up for The Physician Philosopher free email update with each week's posts. You can subscribe to the blog by going to thephysicianphilosopher.com/subscribe

---

[3] Recommended physician finance and wellness websites: https://thephysicianphilosopher.com/recommended/websites/

That's it. That's possible, right? You can do this. I promise.

Chapter 3:
Conflicts of Interest

"Doctors and druggists wash each other's hands –
And always have, exactly Nature's plans"
~ Geoffrey Chaucer, The Canterbury Tales

Imagine that someone is telling you about a study that investigated a new pain medication. She tells you that it has the ability to substantially decrease pain in patients after surgery. Then, she informs you that the most up-to-date research compared this new medicine to the current standard and showed that it was head and shoulders better than what is currently out there. Both statistical and clinical significance were proven. In fact, patients that took this pain medication would often go home without requiring a prescription for opioids. The person saying all of this then advised you that it would probably be best practice to incorporate this new medication into your post-operative pain pathway for surgery. That sounds pretty reasonable, right?

What if you then found out that the paper was paid for by the pharmaceutical company that made the drug and that the person saying all of these wonderful things about the research was a pharmaceutical representative from that company? Would that make a difference in how you viewed this person's advice?

The answer should be an emphatic "*Yes!*" The reason is pretty obvious. Both the study and the person talking about it have a massive conflict of interest. In other words, they are biased. Their advice could be spot on, or their advice could be motivated by self-gain. It's often impossible, or at least very hard, to tell the difference. The one thing we can be sure of is that they stand to make money if we follow their advice.

The same lesson can be applied to the personal finance and insurance industries. We must realize that, as physicians, we have a giant target on our back. People recognize that physicians typically have a high earning capacity and very low financial literacy. The financial industry wants to take a piece of that pie. For this reason, whenever someone is offering financial advice, it is essential to know *exactly* where their conflicts of interest lie during your discussion.

Figure out what's in it for them and how they are getting paid. In fact, you should ask them outright how they make money. It is like playing poker. If, after sitting at the same poker table for some time, you can't figure out who the sucker is ... it's probably you. Ask tough questions. And take a do-it-yourself attitude towards finances when possible. After all, the best person to look out for your own needs and success is YOU!

TPP Conflict of Interest

Before we talk about conflicts in the financial industry, let me first get my own personal conflict of interest out of the way.

I run a website called The Physician Philosopher. It is a for-profit enterprise, generating income mainly through affiliate links, advertisements, and sponsorships. I write in order to help the medical community achieve wealth without forgetting why, which is to live an intentional and balanced life. In order to do this, I have to keep the doors open. Running a successful website certainly isn't free, though I want it to be free for you.

There is nothing on my website that I wouldn't personally recommend or use. But clicking on some of the links could potentially make me money (even if it costs you nothing). That's my only conflict of interest. Everything else in this book is free of any conflict and it's how I operate my personal finances. This is the advice I would give myself if I could turn back the clock.

The Gold Standard for Financial Advising

Before we discuss the conflicts of interest that exist in the financial advising world, let's just get this out there from the beginning. The gold standard for financial advisors checks all of the following boxes. They:
- ❑ Operate as a fiduciary
- ❑ Are a fee-only financial advisor
- ❑ Charge a fair flat fee
- ❑ Have extensive experience working with physicians

Any financial advisor you use should be a fiduciary, which means that they are ethically and legally bound to do what is right for you regardless of whether it makes them more or less money. There should be a signed fiduciary agreement saying as much. This is an absolute must if you decide to use a financial advisor.

Speaking of financial advisors, there are two kinds, fee-based and fee-only advisors. They seem similarly named to intentionally confuse people. Strictly speaking, fee-only financial advisors are different than fee-based financial advisors because they do not offer commissioned products (such as life insurance). An easy way to remember this is that fee "only" advisors are the "only" advisor you should use. In the same way, if you are ever offered a "free" steak dinner you should "only" eat the steak, and avoid buying any products or services from the fee-based advisor offering the dinner. Otherwise, you will not only end up buying your steak, but everyone else's steak, too, whether you realize it or not.

If they don't sell commissioned products, how do fee-only financial advisors make money? The best way is through a flat rate or fee, which is typically charged either hourly or monthly. For example, they may charge a client by the hour to help set up a backdoor Roth. If it takes 2 hours and they charge $150 an hour, then the client would owe them $300. Others will maintain a monthly or annual fee to retain their services. This is exactly how it should be done, because it is straightforward and transparent. They provide you a service and you cut them a check.

Another way that fee-only advisors get paid is by selling a specific financial product. Say, you need a comprehensive financial plan. A fee-only advisor may estimate that it will take 20 hours to create this, and at $150 an hour the financial plan will cost you $3,000. If it takes longer than 20 hours, the good ones eat the cost. Again, this is straightforward. You pay them, you get what you paid for, and that's the end of that.

In this revenue model, there is little to no conflict of interest. The advisor wants their clients to do well so that clients come back for more of their services, if they should need it. The big difference is that they do not make money from the insurance products that they sell you or the assets they could manage. They are fee-only advisors with a flat rate.

It probably goes without saying, but the advisor should also have extensive experience working with physicians. Our financial situation is unique. Whereas most people gradually increase their income, physicians go from low income with high debt to high-income with high debt very quickly. This poses specific problems for us. If you need an advisor, it is important to find out how much experience they have.

Flat fee versus Assets Under Management

Unfortunately, it gets a little more complicated, which is why a fee-only advisor is not the only recommendation listed above. Both fee-based and fee-only advisors can operate in one of two ways: the flat-fee model described above or a fee structure called Assets Under Management (AUM). This is important to understand. Stick with me. We will use this example later in this book.

In AUM models, the industry standard is that the financial advisor gets paid 1% of money managed annually. This doesn't sound like a lot. Many people look at that number and think, "*They want to manage my money and I get to keep 99% and the financial advisor only gets 1% so I can sleep at night? What a steal!*" As Lee Corso would say, "*Not so fast, my friend.*"

For example, let's say you have $1,000,000 split between an IRA and a taxable account (401K/403B holdings are not usually included in AUM fees) managed by a financial advisor. You will pay your advisor $10,000 for managing your money that year, even if your accounts lose money. This doesn't come from your bank account, because who would write a $10,000 check for someone to manage their money? It comes from the assets in your accounts. You never see it leave, but it will have a profound impact on your financial success.

The more money that is managed, the more expensive it gets. If you have $3,000,000 and the advisor's AUM fee is 1%, you can now expect to pay $30,000 each year. Advisors will often have a graded system where they lower the AUM fees once their client has more money to manage. Even if they lower it to 0.5%, you are still paying $15,000 to manage your $3,000,000 saved. That is a lot of money! In a retirement lasting 30-years, this will cost them millions of dollars. That's millions with an "s".

Knowing where your money is going is not the only reason understanding the AUM model is important. AUM models can also introduce massive conflicts of interest. For example, a big conflict of interest exists for a financial advisor operating under an AUM if their client changes jobs and asks them "*What should I do with the money in my current 401K?*"

How does this 401K question expose a conflict of interest? When people change jobs they have three choices: (1) leave the money with their prior employer's 401K (if allowed), (2) roll the 401K into a rollover Investment Retirement Account (IRA), or (3) roll it into their new employer's 401K. Remember, the AUM does not normally include 401K money. It certainly does include money held in IRAs or taxable accounts. An advisor operating under an AUM model may be inclined to tell the person to put the money into a rollover IRA so that the advisor can collect 1% on that money. A rollover IRA prevents this person from taking part in a Backdoor Roth IRA because of the *pro rata rules* – a rule that will increase your taxes if you have other IRA money when performing a Backdoor Roth IRA. Yet, the advisor still may be inclined to recommend this because of the potential to earn more money. Do you see the problem here? It's just like the pharmaceutical rep example. How do you know whether to trust the advice or not?

AUM models produce other conflicts of interest. Any decision that puts less money into the investment accounts that the advisor is managing leads to a conflict for them. Examples include:
- Preferentially paying down student loans instead of investing
- Investing in real estate
- Paying off your mortgage or car loans faster
- Taking social security at age 70 (where you get paid more) instead of age 62
- Investing in a personal business
- Increasing charitable contributions

AUM advisors don't get paid if their clients do any of these things; therefore, they are conflicted and prone to give bad advice. I am not saying that good people can't fight against this model when the temptation arises, but why use the fee-based or AUM models when a less conflicted, fee-only advisory model with a flat rate exists?

This conversation would be incomplete if I didn't give at least a small out for financial advisors operating under an AUM model. If you are reading this book, you are unlikely to benefit from an AUM advisor. That said, there are people who exist in this world who want literally nothing to do with their finances. They want to outsource this just like they do their lawn or child care. In this situation, an AUM advisor is going to be worth every penny because they will prevent this person from making catastrophic behavioral finance decisions, like selling in a down market. That alone would cover their cost. However, if you are willing to spend the time learning the 20% you need to know to get 80% of the results you want, an AUM advisor is not what I'd recommend. Go with a fee-only advisor operating as a fiduciary under a flat-rate payment model who has experience working with physicians, if you need help.

A Brief Primer on Roboadvisors

It is worth mentioning that traditional financial advisory services are not the only source for investment advice. Recently, roboadvisors have entered the landscape. They are called "robo" advisors because they automatically control your investment choices. These "robotic" advisors will rebalance your portfolio, save you taxes when you lose money in a taxable account (e.g., tax-loss harvesting), and can place your money into a portfolio that is suited for your risk tolerance.

Some hybrid models also exist where you can use the automated "robo" service in addition to having access to a financial advisor. Examples of roboadvisor services include the Vanguard Personal Advisory Service, Betterment, and Wealthfront. These services usually follow an AUM fee-structure, which was discussed above. The costs are not inconsequential – usually around 0.25 to 0.5% of the assets being managed – but they are typically less expensive than the traditional financial advisory AUM model.

Commission as a Conflict

In the chapter on asset protection, I will share a story about how I was badly burned by an insurance agent (a.k.a. insurance salesman). The guy that burned me was the brother of one of my medical school classmates. My classmate is a friend of mine to this day, though I've never told him this story. Even if the person who wants to sell you insurance is a "good guy", he can still hurt you. It may not even be intentional; it's just a conflict of interest. This conflict is caused by commissions.

Insurance agents (and fee-based advisors who sell insurance products) get paid by commission. The idea should be familiar even if you aren't aware of it. For example, if you buy tennis shoes from an athletics store at the mall, the person who sells you the shoes usually gets a kickback for getting you to purchase the shoes. (Maybe that's why they call it a "kickback"?) In the same way, insurance agents—who sometimes like to masquerade as financial advisors—make commission off the products people purchase from them.

Why does this matter? The products that provide the highest commission to the insurance agent are likely to get pushed harder; even if they are not the right products for clients. In fact, that's likely the reason they have such a high commission. Otherwise, these lesser products would not be sold. The most common and necessary example of this is whole (or cash-value) life insurance. Here is some solid advice: never mix insurance and investments.

Yet, this perfectly describes whole life insurance, which is a mixture of insurance and investments. Do yourself a favor and just don't fall for it. It's worth repeating that statement: **Don't buy whole life insurance**. That's certainly part of the 20% you need to know. And also trust that the insurance agent will be paid handsomely (50-110% of the first annual premium, which can be as high as $20,000-40,000) when they sell a plan. This is why some insurance agents make it sound like the perfect product for everyone, even children.

Other examples of commission-based products include term life insurance (this is the kind you want), disability insurance (also necessary), and—in the financial advisor world—placing your investments into loaded mutual funds that provide a kickback (not good).

What is the flat fee-only version of insurance salesmen? They are called independent insurance agents (note: not fee-based advisors) that work specifically with physicians. While they still earn a commission from selling you products, they are the least conflicted source. "Independent" agent means someone who can gather quotes from multiple companies. Agents who work for a single insurance company are limited to that company's products. They cannot shop around for you and, even if they could it is not profitable for them to do so. This can pose a serious problem, particularly in the world of disability insurance, where the definition of disability is many different shades of grey.

Take Home

The take home here is pretty simple: If someone is offering advice (particularly advice that has to do with money), do your due diligence and figure out their conflict of interest. Most people giving advice on money or financial products have one. In other words, ask them very specifically how they get paid for their services. Otherwise, you might find yourself with a lot less money, resources, and insurance than you may need.

As Dr. Jim Dahle, the White Coat Investor, would say, *"The main difficulty with choosing an investment advisor is that by the time you know enough to choose a good one, you probably know enough to do your financial planning and asset management on your own."*

For financial advisors, here is your gold-standard checklist:
- ❏ Fee-only
- ❏ Fiduciary
- ❏ Flat-fee model
- ❏ Experience working with physicians

For the insurance industry:
- ❑ Independent insurance agent (not tied to a specific company)
- ❑ Experience working with physicians
- ❑ Less than 1% of their clients have a whole life insurance policy
- ❑ Does not sell annuities

Chapter 4: Financial Choices in Medical School

*"You're braver than you believe,
and stronger than you seem,
And smarter than you think."*
~ Christopher Robin to Winnie-the-Pooh (in *Pooh's Grand Adventure*)

Every medical student remembers hearing that the first year of medical school is like "trying to drink out of a fire hydrant." For me, the struggle was real in the first year of medical school because of this phenomenon. The information was plentiful and often overwhelming. Prior to my first year in medical school, everything came naturally to me. All of a sudden, I was finding out who was the cream of the crop, and it wasn't me anymore.

I struggled so badly in my early training that I was 103 out of 119 following the completion of second year. Third year was about the time that I hit my stride and found out that clinical medicine was my strength. After that year, I found myself no longer on the bottom of the totem pole and finished in the top quartile. Things only improved from there as I became the student body president, and then a chief resident. Let this story give you hope that you, too, can make it!

The reason that I mention this story is to say that I remember the stress of medical school. Adding a major financial burden on top of that stress can suffocate students. Let this chapter serve as a source of information to help ease that stress. Remember, all of the stuff in this book is important, but your job in medical school is to learn. So, this chapter should fill you in on the 20% you need to know (to accomplish 80% of the results). That way you will be able to focus on your real job: learning medicine.

A Word on Financial Education

Most residency programs are designed to do one thing: produce good clinicians. Very rarely do they teach you much in the way of the business of medicine or personal finance. When I say business of medicine, I mean things like billing and coding, starting a practice, managing overhead in a practice, meeting CMS requirements, and things of that nature. If you plan to go the private practice route, you should sort this stuff out. Get that education from someone. At residency interviews, ask if the curriculum adequately covers these topics.

As for personal finance, this may also fall squarely on your shoulders. A lot of residency programs simply do not teach about money. With the long and fabled history of how terrible doctors are with money, this isn't surprising. Most doctors couldn't teach about personal finance even if they wanted to do so. So, what is a medical student or resident to do?

You should educate yourself by reading a few books, including this one. A great time to do this is in your fourth year of medical school after interviews are complete and before you start your internship. Some other books that I'd recommend are the following (all written by physicians, except the last one):

❏ *The White Coat Investor Book* by James M. Dahle, MD (practicing emergency doctor)
❏ *The Doctor's Guide* series by Cory S. Fawcett, MD (Retired surgeon)
❏ *The Investor's Manifesto* by William J. Bernstein, MD (a retired neurologist)
❏ *How to Think About Money* by Jonathan Clements

The books listed above are pretty short reads, maybe with the exception of *The Investor's Manifesto* (but it's a great book). They can be read in less than 5-10 hours and are very digestible.

This probably isn't enough, though. You likely need to continue to maintain your personal finance knowledge base. This can be easily accomplished by reading a few blog posts from physician finance and personal finance websites. This will probably take 5-15 minutes per week. Really, not much at all. There is a list of recommended websites on The Physician Philosopher.

Minimizing Debt Should Be Priority Number One

Seventy-five percent of students come out of medical school with student loans. The average student has just under $200,000[4] in student loan debt. Twenty-one percent of students have credit card debt. The vast

---

[4] AAMC Education Debt Manager. 2018-2019. https://members.aamc.org/eweb/upload/aamc-2018-2019-education-debt-manager.pdf Accessed January 25, 2019.

majority of students do not earn money while in school. All of this equates to one single fact: the financial job of a medical student is to minimize debt.

There are a lot of ways to accomplish this goal. But first, let's dispel one of the most common myths surrounding this subject. Surely you have heard someone say, "*It's only a drop in the bucket!*" What they are implying is that one day you will make big attending physician money and this debt will be small in comparison. Naturally, this is total garbage. To prove this, let's use a personal example.

When I was in medical school I had a full-tuition scholarship. I am married to a teacher and she worked full-time up until my fourth year of medical school, when we had our first child. Her take home pay should have covered our living expenses. However, because I was often told "*it's just a drop in the bucket*" I took out every dime of living expenses that I could. Whatever I didn't need, I could give back, right? Unfortunately, that's not how humans work. I borrowed every dollar I could and spent every dime.

That's where our $105,000 in debt came from: about $26,000 in living expenses for four years. This would balloon during training to $150,000. With my wife's graduate school debt, we combined for $200,000 in student loan debt. We should have come out of medical school with zero debt, aside from my wife's graduate school loans. Instead, we came out with a lot of debt because we unnecessarily inflated our lifestyles during training.

For example, we lived in a townhome with two bedrooms even though we didn't have any kids yet. The second room could have been rented out, but that would have made too much sense. Then, we purchased a house my second year of medical school. And we drove cars that we were making payments on, invested in actively managed funds that we later sold, and ate out far too often while we were in debt. Our bad lifestyle decisions cost us $150,000 in the end. We were making choices that we couldn't afford, which is all too common in today's culture.

Maybe your situation isn't quite the same as mine. Let's look at a different example: say you are trying to decide whether to split an apartment with a classmate using medical school debt to pay the expense. On your own, the apartment would cost $1,000, and with a roommate it's only $500. That's a potential savings of $6,000 per year. It would cost you $24,000 over the four years ($6,000 x 4 years) of medical school to live alone. However, we are forgetting something we introduced earlier: the interest on the debt. From the day you make your decision, the loaned money you use for living expenses will accumulate interest. If the loans are at 6.5% interest, how much will your choice to live alone cost by the time you start paying off loans as an attending? The answer is that the $24,000 initial cost will grow into just under $38,000. All because you wanted to live alone during medical school. That's an expensive decision.

The point here isn't that you should live with a roommate. The point is that if you can save yourself $500 per month, you are saving yourself $38,000 in debt when you finish training. Minimizing debt matters in the end. Maybe that means not having a car payment, living in a more affordable place, having a roommate, living with your parents, or not eating out everyday for lunch and dinner. Save where you can, but realize that every dollar you spend now will be ~$1.50 later. If the rate on your loans is higher than the 6.5% in the example above, every $1 will be more like $2 later.

The other myth that must be dispelled is the argument *"When I am an attending physician, this won't seem like a lot of debt."* That's garbage, too. As an attending I would now go up and buy my old self a six pack of beer every week if I would have stopped making stupid decisions and minimized my debt. There was no reason for us to have debt after medical school and about three reasons why we should have had zero. Hopefully, you'll learn this lesson sooner than I did!

Do your future self a favor and don't make dumb decisions. You are smart. You got into medical school. Do the right thing. Your future self will thank you.

Should I use borrowed money to go to the Super Bowl?

We are about to discuss some high-yield topics, but before we do I need to convince you of why it is important to live within your means during medical school and residency – in case I haven't already accomplished that goal.

I've been asked before whether it is a good idea to use borrowed money to pay for an expensive vacation or to attend a rare event (such as a sporting event). This is an impossible question to answer from a wellness perspective. How happy would this trip make the person? How long would that happiness last? How much money is that happiness worth? I don't know the answer to these questions, because everyone is different.

That said, there is a mathematical answer to the question. Using borrowed money has a cost and we can make some pretty good assumptions at how much it will cost. As an example, let's use a $3,000 trip to New York that my wife and I took right after Step 1 of the USMLE (and well before I knew anything about money). How much did this trip cost us from an investment and debt perspective? Given my view on investing through passive index funds (more on this later), let's take that $3,000 and put it into Vanguard's Total Stock Market Index Fund (VTSMX). We took this trip in April of 2010, but would have paid for it likely in February or March of 2010. On February 19, 2010, the VTSMX was valued at $27.50. At the time of this writing, the value is $67.32, which is approximately 2.448 times the February 2010 value. Therefore, my $3,000 would be worth **$7,334** (as of of early 2018). Every day my debt is not paid off, that trips costs me more.

However, I don't think this is the best way to look at it. The money used for that trip came from medical school debt for living expenses that would later become my student loan debt burden. So, how much additional debt has that cost me? Assuming my 6.8% interest during medical school, residency, and fellowship, this $3,000 cost me about $5,000. I ended up paying almost double what the trip cost.

Was that trip that I purchased with borrowed money worth it? That's much tougher to say. That's one more month of student loans. One more month until financial independence. We did have a bunch of fun on that trip, though. Weigh that against being debt free, and I am not sure what to tell you. Regardless, my job is to give you the information so that you can make an intentional decision. Every borrowed dollar you spend in medical school will cost you 1.5-2 times as much when you pay it off. Make sure it is truly worth it for you.

Practical Principles for Minimizing Debt

There are a lot of ways to minimize debt. Some of them even include the opposite, which is to make money during medical school.

The big three

Your living expenses have a lot to do with minimizing your debt. It's almost always the "big three" expenses—your house, transportation, and food—that sink people in the debt arena. Is there a way to flip the script on some of these? The car is pretty simple: drive the least expensive car that accomplishes your goals. I discuss this in the next chapter. For food? Well, for starters, don't eat out every day. And if you eat out expensively, definitely don't do it every month. Bring your lunch and your coffee most days. Cook at home. This will save you more money than you think. David Bach made this idea famous in his book, *The Latte Factor* (one latte a day may not seem like much, but it costs you quite a bit compounding over multiple years).

What's the trick for housing? I've already shared it. Split the cost of the house/apartment with a roommate or two. Consider living with family, if possible.

State forgiveness programs

We will talk about Public Service Loan Forgiveness (PSLF) in a later chapter. PSLF is a federal program open to residents of all states. This is not the only option for student loan forgiveness. Another option that is commonly overlooked, but is designed to help out with student loans, are state forgiveness program(s).

For example, in North Carolina there is a Forgivable Education Loans Service (FELS). The FELS program is meant to help ease the student loan debt burden for North Carolina residents who plan to work in North Carolina following the completion of their training. You must be in a qualified profession (being a physician is one of them). If you promise to work as an attending physician in North Carolina for four years after you complete your training, the program will pay $14,000 per year while you are in medical school ($56,000 in total loan forgiveness). It essentially works as a scholarship to medical school that you promise to pay back by working in the state when you finish. One hack here is that if you apply for a full license while in training—and you are training in the state where you "owe your time"—some of your training time can be counted. Some residents that I work with will only owe one year of service to North Carolina when they finish their training because they paid back three years during anesthesiology residency.

Like many programs, you must notify the FELS program within 90 days of graduation from medical school that you plan to use the program for forgiveness. FELS forgiveness is tax free, which is *not* always the case with other "forgiveness" programs! So, check into your state's forgiveness program before you end up with a large and unexpected tax bill.

Many of you are not North Carolina residents. That's okay; many states have programs like this. Don't miss these opportunities because you don't know about them. Do your homework and check into the specific options available in your state.

Many states also have other programs that focus on primary care specialities. In California, the California State Loan Repayment Program (SLRP) will forgive up to $50,000 in loans for primary care specialties. As part of this program, the practice where you work must be willing to match the forgiveness dollar for dollar. This forgiveness certainly should help to provide more primary care doctors to the state of California. Like the North Carolina FELS program, the debt forgiven through California SLRP is tax exempt.

Before you privately refinance, you should consider these options in your decision tree. Once you have privately refinanced or consolidated your debt with a spouse, you often no longer qualify for state and federal forgiveness programs. Be sure to gather all of the information for your situation and then do your due diligence and make an intentional decision.

Military programs

While I am not an expert on this subject matter, I want you to know that this option exists. I am the first male in three or four generations not to serve in the U.S. military. Part of me has always felt an obligation to do so at some point.   For some serving our country is a calling, and for other it can also serve to help you pay your student loans.

Potential benefits:
- A substantial sign-on bonus is often included.
- You will receive a monthly stipend during medical school.
- The military will pay for your medical school loans.
- You will have the opportunity to serve your country.

Drawbacks to consider:
- The country owns your time after you finish medical school.
- You owe one year of service for each year paid for by the military.
- You have less choice about specialty—it depends more on the military's needs and less on your preferences.
- The math may favor a civilian route depending on your specialty and debt burden.
- You may be deployed. Your thoughts on this possibility may change depending on your family situation (or lack thereof).

Whatever you decide, do your homework. Realize that this is an option, but not one to be taken lightly. Ultimately, the decision to serve your country will not be a strictly financial decision. Considerable thought should be put into this decision prior to pulling the trigger.

Take Home

One other critical point to mention before we get to our take home is that **you should file your taxes as a fourth year medical student**, even if you have a zero dollar income. This will allow you to enroll in the income-driven repayment programs we will discuss in a later chapter.

Live like a medical student while you are in medical school. Do this by:
- Minimizing your debt, particularly when it comes to houses, cars, and food.
- Make sure to take advantage of anything that will allow you to live more frugally while balancing your needs.
- Recognize that every $1 you spend in medical school will cost you $1.50-$2.00 later.
- Look into both state and federal debt forgiveness programs to limit your debt accumulation.
- The military scholarship program is an option, but it is a decision that requires a lot of thought.
- Fourth year students should file their taxes.

Chapter 5:
The Pareto Principle for Residency

"Money is a terrible master, but an excellent servant"
~ P.T. Barnum

The total amount of credit card debt owed by Americans is over $1 trillion. The average household has over $8,000 in credit card debt.[5] This problem exists for residents, too. One study found that 21% of residents had credit card debt,[6] though that number seems low.

The more debt you have, the less money you can use to build wealth. It's a simple math problem. The amount of money residents earn is right at the median income for our country.[7] While your income will most likely increase dramatically once you finish, residents must not lose sight of the big picture. If you are a resident, you are earning as much money as half of the country. For this reason, the question isn't whether it's possible to pay down debt or save during residency.

---

[5] ABC News. Credit card debt surpasses $1 trillion in the US for first time. https://abcnews.go.com/Business/credit-card-debt-surpasses-trillion-us-time/story?id=53608548 Accessed December 15th, 2019.
[6] Ahmad, FA. White AJ, Hiller KM, Amini R, Jeffe DB. An assessment of residents' and fellows' personal finance literacy: an unmet medical education need. Int J Med Educ. 2017; 8:192-204. doi: 10.5116/ijme.5918.ad11.
[7]Wikipedia. https://en.wikipedia.org/wiki/Household_income_in_the_United_States. Accessed January 25th, 2019.

The question is *how* you should pay down debt and save.

I am a firm believer in balancing future goals with the ability to love the life you are currently living. That's the focus of the last chapter of this book and for good reason. So, while I talk about the following ways to minimize the financial pain of residency, please remember to live a little, too. Have some fun. Take some trips. Just be smart about it! This is the 20% you need to know to place yourself on the path to financial success.

Focus on Debt (And Some Interesting Hacks)

The most common question that I get from residents and attendings alike is whether they should be paying down debt or investing. For many, paying down debt and getting a "guaranteed" 5 -7% on their money is the best bet. [By guaranteed, I mean that money paid towards loans is money that you must pay back, and it has a set interest rate. You will get no better or worse than the set rate. So, it is "guaranteed". This is in opposite to what happens when you invest in the market where you have an equal chance to make or lose money on what you invest.] This isn't the case for everyone, though.

Here are four groups of people who would benefit from investing some money during residency:

1. People who don't have any medical school debt
   Twenty-five percent of graduating medical

students do not have any medical school debt. Maybe you have a military scholarship, a full ride, a big 529, or generous parents/grandparents. Regardless of the source, if you are in this subset of residents and have no other debt, then by all means you should be investing during residency.

2. People who are enrolled in Revised Pay As You Earn (REPAYE) and receive a subsidy
You need to choose between paying more (and having less subsidized and paid by the government) or investing money into a retirement account. If your subsidy is high, investing may be a better option. It may also decrease your gross income if invested pre-tax, which will lower your monthly payment in REPAYE and increase the subsidy.

3. If you get a benefit from investing, such as a 401K/403B match (Note: ask about how money is vested at your institution – in other words, if you get to keep the money when you leave residency).
In this scenario, you are leaving money on the table if you do not invest.

4. If you get a tax break from investing, such as a "saver's tax credit"
If you are single, you likely do not earn a "saver's tax credit" after your intern year for putting money into an IRA. Many married couples might qualify, depending on how much each spouse earns. If you qualify for the tax credit, invest that amount of money into an IRA ($2,000 single; $4,000 married) to get the maximum tax credit.

Many of you reading this book should simply take the guaranteed return on paying off your loans. If you don't meet one of the criteria above, don't invest money in the market that may or may not do better than the 5-7% you are losing on your student loans.

Don't Ignore Your Debt

One of the worst financial mistakes I made during residency was to ignore my debt. I went into forbearance on my debt every year. Forbearance and deferment should be last resort options that are the best choice for almost no one. It's the easy way out, but almost never the right thing. I mention it here, because technically it is "an option," but it's almost never the right one. Just don't do it. Ignorance is not bliss. You need to make a plan.

The next two chapters will spell out the specifics on what a student loan debt plan should look like. Suffice it to say here, you absolutely must make an intentional plan to pay down your debt. The best time to do this is during the fourth year of medical school or in the first few months as an intern. The later you wait, the longer compound interest is your foe.

Consumer Debt (Credit Cards)

Unfortunately, student loan debt is not the only debt we need to discuss. Consumer debt from credit cards is a pretty big problem. It is not uncommon for a resident to tell me that they have $5,000 or $10,000 in credit card debt. Credit card debt is usually a behavioral finance problem. Most of the time, it is not a lack of income problem. Debt is not normal no matter what our culture and society teach you.

Those new designer jeans or expensive sunglasses likely won't make you any happier than the ones you already have. Going skiing in the Alps sounds great, but you could probably just go somewhere closer during residency, right? Will the fun in the Alps be worth all the additional debt compared to the lower cost choice? Learn the art of being content with what you have in residency and just after. That may be the most important thing you learn from this book.

A brief mention on travel hacking

Don't take my comments on credit card debt the wrong way. I am not anti-credit cards. I use credit cards as tool to gain cash back and points. For example, we use one credit card for gas (3% back) and groceries (2% back) and another for everything else to give us points to travel. When we fly, we fly free. That's travel hacking.

Here's the most important point about using credit cards: use them just like debit cards. Pay cash on them every month and pay the full amount. I've never carried a balance on a credit card one month that rolled over to the next. If you can't pay off the total bill each month, you shouldn't have a credit card. Credit cards are tools. However, if you can't control your urge to spend when you cannot afford something, they are going to hurt you more than they help. If you wouldn't (or can't) pay with cash for something, don't put it on a credit card.

If you can use credit cards as a tool, this can be a powerful way to travel hack for all of those residency, fellowship, and job interviews. Free flights save you a lot of money, and, if you were going to spend the money anyway to buy bread and milk, what's the downside?

As a brief primer on travel hacking, the idea is to continue to spend the (low) amount of money that you currently spend from your budget (remember, you are supposed to budget). Instead of using a debit card that provides no benefits, use a credit card with reward points. You build points/miles on the card and then use those to travel when the need arises. The important part is that this is money you *would have spent anyway*. Don't use rewards as an excuse to purchase items you cannot afford.

There are a lot of websites out there that discuss this topic in greater detail. I'll point you to one of my favorite sources, which is from a fellow physician finance blogger, Physician on Fire (Physicianoonfire.com).

One other thing about credit card hacking. The 5/24 rule for some credit card companies (Chase being the most notable) limits you from getting more than 5 credit cards in a 24-month period. So, don't get carried away! Do your research and pick the best card for you.

Revisiting the Rule of 72

We have discussed the necessity of having a primary focus on debt, but if you are in one of the four groups who should consider investing, you may need some help.

Before we talk specifics, I need to convince you that investing is worthwhile during training. We are going to keep this one simple. Let's assume a typical retirement timeline. In this example, you work 30 years after you finish training and you are retired for another 30 before you die. That's a total of 60 years. What is the end value of every $100 you save during residency and invest into a Roth IRA (which should be the money you touch last in retirement) assuming 6% compound interest? Using the Rule of 72, we can figure that number will double every 12 years (72/6 = 12). Your money will double five times in 60 years.

Every $100 you invested during residency would grow to $1,600 in 60 years. Every $1,000 would be worth $16,000. If you maxed out your IRA ($5,500) each year over a four-year training period, you can expect to have over $415,000 after 60 years. That's a lot of money! For this reason, don't minimize the impact of even small amounts of money invested in the market during residency. Time in the market is the most important aspect of investing.

As an example, look at the following graph, which you will see more than once. Notice how all of the savings a person has are first determined by their savings rate (dark bar on the left) before the interest finally takes over (lighter bar) and accounts for the majority after about 17 years of contributions. Your savings rate is the major determinant of your investing success early on! Every bit counts.

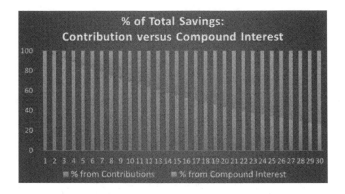

% of Total Savings:
Contribution versus Compound Interest

Should I Buy or Rent a House?

One of the most common questions fourth year medical students ask is "*Should I buy or rent during residency?*" The short answer is easy. Renting is usually the better option. Why? There are a few reasons.

First, the time it takes after buying a house to have enough equity in a home – or current value above what is owed on the mortgage - that it wouldn't cost you money to sell it is on average at least four years and often more. For example, it takes more than 18 years to break even in New York City.[8] Given the short and definable length of residency training, buying a house probably doesn't fit into this timeline for most parts of the country. For this reason, when you go to sell your home, it will usually cost you money. Brokers and realtors do not work for free.

---

[8] CNBC. Here's how long it takes to break even when you buy a house in 11 major US cities. https://www.cnbc.com/2017/04/12/how-long-it-takes-to-break-even-on-a-house-in-11-major-us-cities.html Accessed January 25th, 2019.

Second, when people compare their monthly mortgage payment to the higher payment it would take to rent, they are comparing apples and oranges. Buying a house requires down payments and locked-in money, not to mention that the cost of home ownership is about more than the monthly payment. Other expenses must be considered, including property tax, upkeep, and yard/lawn maintenance. I bet you didn't count that in the cost, and it's certainly not a fair comparison to renting if you don't. Yes, monthly rent is usually higher, but the property manager will likely pay the property tax and mow the lawn. If the water heater or air conditioner breaks, the property manager is on the hook to pay for the repair. As a homeowner, you'd get to swallow those costs yourself.

Third, unless you stay at the same place where you trained, you likely do not know the area well enough to know that the house you just bought is where you want to live or that it will serve as a good investment 3-5 years later. Will you be able to turn around and sell it three to five years? As I mentioned above, selling a house is expensive and you certainly wouldn't want to incur the 10% of the house cost it takes to sell a home. Our goal is to build wealth, and this would accomplish the opposite.

After reading the considerations above, you may still feel inclined to buy a house. It's the American dream, after all! As always, I encourage you to do your homework and to make an intentional decision. Recognize that a house you own feels very similar to a house that you don't. They will both have a front door and a place to sleep. Don't get caught in the trappings of being a homeowner. It's not all it's cracked up to be.

There are some situations where buying a house is the right thing to do. For example, in my program there is a resident who is—along with his wife—skilled at updating and "flipping" houses. He is using this skillset to flip his current house when he moves. He will likely make a large profit selling his house after just four years. I am sure that there are other examples and times where buying a house is the right move; generally speaking, though, it is not the best decision for residents.

Buying a Car

Remember this sage advice: When you are a resident, you should not live like an attending. In fact, you are going to read here in a little bit that I actually recommend you not only live like a resident during residency, but that you continue to do so for the first 2-3 years after you finish.

A resident's car needs to do exactly three things: 1) get them from point A to point B, 2) get them to their location safely, and 3) be dependable. If your car fails to do any of those three things, then the car probably isn't going to cut it. That said, there are A LOT of cars out there that accomplish those three jobs and don't break the bank. They usually cost $5,000-$10,000.

Also, it is worth mentioning that there is evidence out there that suggests that buying a new car will not make you any happier.[9] As a car guy, it really pains me to say that. But it's true. A nicer car will feel like "just a car" when you have been awake for 24 hours on call. It's not going to feel any different than the $5,000 beater. Why? Because the nice car doesn't change your situation. And, also, because your beater will accomplish the three critical jobs just as well as a brand new BMW.

Moonlighting

Some residencies will afford you the opportunity to moonlight and earn some side income while in training. I did this during my third and fourth year in anesthesia residency and doubled my salary. Unfortunately, that occurred during my financial dark times where I knew nothing about money. I had a 401K available to me, but didn't check to see if they had a match, and when I left that moonlighting gig I took it all out instead of rolling it into my next employer's plan. This cost me 10% of the money plus taxes.

Moonlighting income can be paid to you either as an independent contractor (under a 1099 form) or as an employee (under a W-2 form). If you are paid as an independent contractor, you can opt to open up an independent 401K, which is sometimes called a "solo 401K." As discussed elsewhere, this is preferable to a Simplified Employee Pension (SEP) IRA, because the

[9] Zhang JW, Howell RT, Caprariello PA, Guevarra DA. Damned if they do, damned if they don't: Material buyers are not happier from material or experiential consumption. https://doi.org/10.1016/j.jrp.2014.03.007

solo 401K will allow you to still contribute to a backdoor Roth IRA when you become an attending.

As an employee, your employer pays the employer side of Federal Insurance Contributions Act (FICA) taxes, or Social Security and Medicare, while you are responsible for the employee FICA taxes. However, if you are paid as an independent contractor, you are considered self-employed, which means you will pay both the employee and employer side of the FICA tax (self-employment tax). If you are fortunate enough to earn more than the Social Security wage base ($132,900 for 2019), you will no longer owe that tax from the employee side regardless of whether you are an employee or contractor. This will increase your take-home paycheck by 6.2%. As an attending, this will likely happen every year. This bump in pay is not a mistake; it simply means you have fully paid into the Social Security system for the year and no longer need to pay that tax.

One other note in this primer on moonlighting. If you work as an independent contractor, you can write off business expenses like white coats or medical equipment (shoes for work, stethoscopes, etc.). This is one advantage of being "self-employed." If you itemize your taxes, you should make sure to take advantage of that opportunity. I realize that you are unlikely to itemize as a resident, particularly with the increased federal deductions provided in 2019, but it is worth mentioning here. The same opportunity exists if you ever get paid as an independent contractor as an attending (for example, if you worked locums tenens shifts).

Take Home

Hopefully, this chapter has proven the necessity of living like a resident and provided some tools to do help you do so.

Here are the takeaways:
- Keep student loan and consumer debt down.
- Make an intentional plan to get rid of debt, if you have it.
- Invest in the market during residency if you find yourself in the right situation. Invest in a Roth IRA or in your pre-tax employer plan if you get a match.
- Stick to the plan and review it if you ever feel the need to stray.
- Use the tools that you have at your disposal to get ahead—or, at the very minimum, do not put yourself further behind.
- Use credit cards to travel hack where you can, but only if you can control your urges to buy.
- Moonlight if it's available to you and take advantage of any benefits offered there.

Chapter 6:
Student Loan Debt Management Part 1: Income-driven Repayment and Public Service Loan Forgiveness Programs

Interest never sleeps nor sickens nor dies; it never goes to the hospital; it works on Sundays and holidays; it never takes a vacation; it never visits nor travels; it takes no pleasure ... it has no expense of living; it has neither weddings nor births nor deaths; it has no love, no sympathy; it is as hard and soulless as a granite cliff. Once in debt, interest is your companion every minute of the day and night; you cannot shun it or slip away from it; you cannot dismiss it; it yields neither to entreaties, demands, or orders; and whenever you get in its way or cross its course or fail to meet its demands, it crushes you.
~ J. Reuben Clark, in 1938

I remember the first time a resident of mine told me that she had more than half a million dollars in debt. While it pales in comparison to the greater than $1 million dollars that some have in student loan debt, she was still quite overwhelmed. Honestly, she had no idea what to do with this vast amount of money that she owed to someone else. With pressure from their spouse to move to a higher cost of living area, she felt like Atlas—the weight of the world was on her shoulders. This led me, as an academic anesthesiologist, to start asking a pretty simple question: How can I expect my residents and fellows to focus on learning their craft if they felt overwhelmed by their debt burden? This became a central passion of mine in helping my trainees begin to tackle this tough question.

This chapter will help you make a plan to destroy your debt. While each situation is unique, this primer should at least point you in the right direction. It's lengthy and has lots of detail. That said, if you stick with me, the vast majority of you will know exactly what to do with your debt when you finish reading.

We will first discuss the facts surrounding Public Service Loan Forgiveness (PSLF). Students and residents think that they know how this program works, and yet, I hear them say a lot of things that are not true. In fact, more than 70% of applicants were denied from PSLF because they were failing to make qualifying payments as required by the plan.[10]

If you can't stand the details and it bores you, there is a guide at the end of the chapter for specific situations. That said, if you bear with me, you will gain a strong idea of how to handle your student loan debt.

---

[10] Marketwatch. This government loan forgiveness program has rejected 99% of borrowers so far. https://www.marketwatch.com/story/this-government-loan-forgiveness-program-has-rejected-99-of-borrowers-so-far-2018-09-20 Acessed January 25th, 2019.

Public Service Loan Forgiveness (PSLF)

The PSLF program was started in 2007 to help students with debt who were willing to work for qualifying employers. The idea was this: after you make 120 qualifying monthly payments in a qualifying repayment program while working full time (part time doesn't count) for a qualifying employer, your debt is forgiven. And that forgiveness is tax free. Remember, there are three qualifications while working full-time: a qualifying payment, qualifying repayment program, and a qualifying employer. Please, check all three of these boxes.

You should note that there are two types of forgiveness that can be granted by making payments within the Income Drive Repayment (IDR) programs, such as PAYE and REPAYE. The first is forgiveness through PSLF, which is forgiven as a tax-free event *no matter how much is owed*. This is a stark contrast to the other option that exists; receiving forgiveness directly from the IDR programs after making payments for 20-25 years. This type of "forgiveness" is a taxable event. Who would want to pay taxes on an additional $300,000 or even $1,000,000 worth of taxable income? Not this guy. I don't suppose you would either, but I must admit that this is the right thing to do for a few select groups of people (i.e. those with massive debt-to-income ratios who aren't able to take part in PSLF, but still make payments in the Income Drive Repayment programs). You should know that option exists.

Who should consider PSLF?

If your debt-to-income ratio is ≥ 1, you should really give PSLF a lot of consideration. For example, if your anticipated salary as an attending will be $250,000, you should consider PSLF if you have greater than (or equal to) $250,000 in student loan debt. The more lopsided that ratio becomes (more debt, lower income) the more PSLF becomes a must. If you are ≥ 2 on the ratio ($500,000 debt; $250,000 income), it would be really foolish not to try to do PSLF.

You might also consider PSLF if you have a longer training paradigm. For example, if you are a neurosurgery resident/fellows and have a 7- to 8-year training period, you might as well do PSLF. Assuming that you make small PSLF payments while in training, you only need to make payments for a couple of years as an attending to have it all forgiven. Same goes for those who pursue interventional cardiology (3 years internal medicine + 3 years cardiology fellowship + 1 year of interventional fellowship) or anyone else with a longer training period. Interestingly, this is the reason that most people who are enrolled in PSLF are specialists, and not primary care doctors.

Let's discuss the three qualifications that are required for this program:

Qualifying employer

The biggest misconception I find among residents is that they believe that most hospitals do not qualify for PSLF. This is actually far from the truth. More than

70% of hospitals qualify for PSLF.[11] However, this does not imply that 70% of doctors qualify. You must be an employee at the qualifying hospital. If you are a private practice doctor who contracts with a qualifying hospital, but you are paid by your practice, you do not qualify. This is common among emergency medicine and anesthesiology physicians.

Many residents will ultimately become hospital employees. If you are a hospital employee, there is a >70% chance that your employer qualifies for PSLF. This includes both academic and non-academic medical centers. For this reason, please don't rule PSLF out as an option until you absolutely must.

How do so many hospitals qualify? Well, 70% of the hospitals in this country meet one of the following criteria:
- 501(c)3 non-profit organizations[12]
- Governmental agencies and departments (public/state colleges and universities)

While there are exceptions to the criteria listed above, those two classifications are the most common reasons that employers qualify for PSLF. Regardless, once you decide where to work and whether you will be a hospital employee, you should find out if your employer qualifies.

---

[11] 2018-2019 AAMC Education Debt Manager. https://members.aamc.org/eweb/upload/aamc-2018-2019-education-debt-manager.pdf Accessed January 25th, 2019.
[12] If interested in searching for organizations, look here: https://www.irs.gov/charities-non-profits/tax-exempt-organization-search

It is best practice to submit the paperwork to recertify your employer each year to make sure they are still a PSLF qualifying employer. Technically you only need to recertify when you change employers, but it certainly doesn't hurt. Hospitals can change their filing status each year. If your employer becomes a for-profit enterprise, recertifying each year will save you the pain of finding out (years later) that your payments never qualified.

Qualifying payments

Not all payments count for PSLF, unfortunately. The payments must be on the right kind of loans, after the program started, under a qualifying payment plan (more below), while you are working full time for a qualifying employer.

Your loans must be federal direct loans, but don't worry if all of your loans are not direct loans. Loans can often be consolidated to become eligible for PSLF. However, you must consolidate before you make PSLF payments. Otherwise, you lose credit after you consolidate. It should also be mentioned that Parent PLUS loans and private loans are excluded in any form, regardless of whether they are consolidated.

Additionally, if you consolidate loans, you will lose the grace period. However, this is a good thing as you want to make as many payments during internship as possible when your payment is low (if your household earns no income during medical school, your qualifying payment may be zero dollars). It should be mentioned that if you consolidate after you have made payments towards PSLF, the clock starts all over again. So, consolidate early, if that is the route you choose to take.

Qualifying repayment programs

There are multiple plans that qualify under PSLF. The two broad categories include the Income-driven Repayment (IDR) programs and the standard repayment program. However, the standard repayment program involves making payments so that your debt is paid over ten years. So, if you start and finish in the standard repayment program, then your forgiven debt is zero dollars. You paid it all. The reason to mention that standard repayment plans qualify is that if you switch out of or into the standard repayment program during your 120 monthly payments, your payments should still qualify. For example, you could pay five years under REPAYE and then five years under the standard repayment program and still receive forgiveness on whatever debt is unpaid after 10 years.

As for the IDR programs, this includes the following four repayment programs: Income Contingent Repayment (ICR), Income Based Repayment (IBR), Pay As You Earn (PAYE), and Revised Pay As You Earn (REPAYE). Each of these programs has different qualifications and features. We will talk about those soon, but before we do there is one giant bone to pick about PSLF. Let's deal with that first.

What if I don't trust PSLF?

This is the most common question that I get about PSLF. Surprisingly, it has nothing to do with recertification, qualifying employers, or even which program to join. The most common question is this: *"What should I do if I don't trust the government to own up on forgiving my debt when I finally make the 120 payments?"* This question has been amplified with some reports that 99% of people have been denied after applying for PSLF.[8] So, what if you don't trust PSLF?

That's a great question. Here's the answer:

Trust, but verify.

It's the same code of arms that the field of anesthesiology embraces. Trust what people tell you, but you better verify it yourself! I can't tell you how many times that has prevented bad outcomes in my line of work. The same goes for PSLF. Trust that the tax-free forgiveness is going to happen, but verify that your plan will work regardless. Why should you trust PSLF? Well, when financial programs are changed by the government, they usually grandfather people in or provide a grace period to those already enrolled. If you are currently in PSLF and have a signed promissory note, do you think that they would sweep away the whole system, including those that are already enrolled?

Your trust is not without risk, given that there has been recent legislation (the PROSPER act) and presidential budgets which have discussed scrapping the PSLF system. A little trust is warranted, but we need to verify the success of our financial plan in case our trust is misplaced and the government reneges on their promise.

How do you verify? Insurance. But not insurance in the form of life, disability, or umbrella insurance. You need insurance through an investment account, such as a taxable account.

Remember, the goal for participants in PSLF is to pay the minimum amount required to have the maximum amount forgiven. We can discuss the ethics of this elsewhere. The rules are the rules. It's our job to play the game. Given that the name of the game is to make minimal payments, you want to pay substantially less than you would have had you refinanced privately and were trying to pay your debt off in 3-5 years.

Here is a stepwise approach to follow once you are an attending physician in PSLF but you don't trust it.
1. Figure out how much your monthly payment would be under private refinancing. Do the math or use and online calculator to determine this.
2. Determine your monthly payment under the appropriate IDR program. (Or look it up if you are already enrolled.)
3. Take the number from 2 and subtract it from the number in 1.
4. Invest this amount in a taxable investment account each month.
5. If the government breaks its promise, use this money to pay off the remaining debt. If they don't, then pat yourself on the back for being that much closer to financial independence.

For example, assume you have a family of four with $250,000 in income and $300,000 in debt refinanced at 3.5% interest over a five-year payment plan.
1. The monthly payment is $5,500.
2. PAYE/REPAYE payments would be right around $1,800 per month.

3. The difference between your monthly payment under a private loan and the IDR payment is $3,700. $5,500-$1,800 = $3,700
4. Invest $3,700 in a taxable account each month. This may require you to live like a resident for the first few years.
5. Enjoy the rewards of being smart and having a plan.

One other note on PSLF: keep all of the documentation and paperwork you ever receive about your loans. If you send anything in the mail, then you should probably send it certified. The government isn't quite as good as you are at keeping track of these things, and there is no reason to lose a payment that "counts" if you can prove it. If you are in PSLF, keep good records.

Income-driven Repayment (IDR) Programs

Now that you know how to make a plan to trust, but verify, PSLF, we will spend some time discussing the Income-driven Repayment (IDR) programs that qualify under PSLF. The four are Revised Pay As You Earn (REPAYE), Pay As You Earn (PAYE), Income-based Repayment (IBR), and Income-contingent Repayment (ICR). PAYE and REPAYE are the best programs. If you don't qualify for these (or if REPAYE doesn't make sense for you), I would weigh the prospect of PSLF with IBR/ICR versus privately refinancing during residency to get a better interest rate. If you have a high debt:-to-income ratio or a long training paradigm, IBR/ICR may be your best option.

Caveat for medical students:

Be sure to file your taxes in your fourth year of medical school. Even if you don't make any money, you will need this information for figuring your income-driven repayment options. As always, save a copy, too.

Before we discuss PAYE and REPAYE, let's review some definitions.

1) **Discretionary income**: In the eyes of the government, discretionary income is income that is not absolutely essential and that you get to choose (with your discretion) how to spend. The strict definition is as follows:

Discretionary income = Adjusted Gross Income (AGI) - 150% of poverty line.

2) **Poverty Line**: The poverty line depends on where you live and the number of people in your household.[13] IDR programs use a percentage of your discretionary income to determine your payment.

2) **Standard Repayment Plan (SRP) Payment**: To find your monthly SRP payment, plug your

---

[13] You can find the 150% poverty lines for the continental U.S. here
http://www.uscourts.gov/sites/default/files/poverty-guidelines.pdf

interest rate and the total amount of debt into the following equation in an Excel sheet:

=PMT(Interest Rate%/12, 120, total debt,0,0)

For example, if you have $200,000 in debt at 6.5% interest, the equation would look like this: =PMT(6.5%/12, 120,200000,0,0). You must add the "%" sign for the equation to work out.

3) **Partial Financial Hardship (PFH)**. In IBR and PAYE, you must prove a PFH in order to be eligible. This is difficult to do as an attending physician, but it can often be done during residency. This will be key later in the plans that I lay out.

If your calculated monthly payment is less under PAYE (or IBR) than under the monthly payment for SRP, then you have a partial financial hardship.

If you want to qualify under PAYE, you qualify for PFH if:

SRP payment > [10% (AGI- 150% poverty line)]

If you want to qualify under IBR, you qualify for PFH if:

SRP payment > [15% (AGI- 150% poverty line)]

Revised Pay as You Earn (REPAYE)

The REPAYE program was a revision of the PAYE program. This revision qualifies more people who did not previously qualify under PAYE. There is a reason that I mention the revised version first. It's simply better than the original (and all of the others) for most people. In fact, it's usually much better than the private refinance options offered during residency as well.

As of July of 2012, graduate students are no longer eligible to receive subsidized federal loans. This is an important distinction, because it means all loans for medical students are now unsubsidized. REPAYE is the only program that will still pay for 50% of any unpaid interest following your monthly payment on unsubsidized loans each month. This is what makes REPAYE really stand out.

I would argue that REPAYE is the best program for almost all residents (assuming you are not married to a high-income earner), even if you don't plan to pursue PSLF.

Pros of REPAYE

- Effective interest rate reduction for both subsidized and unsubsidized loans
  - This is the biggest one. Stick with me. It's important.

- Following your monthly payment (which is often very low in residency), 50% of any remaining unpaid interest is paid for by the U.S. Department of Education regardless of whether it's subsidized or unsubsidized. This feature is unique to REPAYE.
- Assume that you are an intern and your payment is zero dollars, which is often the case if you earned no money during medical school, and that you are accruing $1,000 in interest each month. Following your zero-dollar payment, you will have $500 paid on your behalf, and only $500 will accrue in interest. That is an effective interest rate reduction. It "effectively" cuts your interest rate in half.

- REPAYE interest does not capitalize (your interest doesn't start earning interest) until you leave the program.
- More people qualify. Essentially, anyone with federal direct loans (or those that consolidate to these loans) qualifies. This isn't true for many other programs.
- It is usually much cheaper than the standard 10-year repayment plan.
- Your REPAYE payment is 10% of your discretionary income.

Cons of REPAYE

- You don't qualify for REPAYE if you have Parent PLUS or FFEL loans (or consolidated loans with Parent PLUS loans).

- The total monthly payment under REPAYE is not capped. It continually rises with increasing income. So, while your discretionary income is low (i.e., during residency), REPAYE is a great plan. When your discretionary income is high (i.e., as an attending) this is not so good.
- Your spouse's income is considered regardless of how you file your taxes. This means that REPAYE is often not the best plan if you are married to a high-income earner (>$100,000). You'll have to do the math to see if you are still getting any forgiveness through the program with a higher AGI. If not, then PAYE is a better option. More on that below.
- Capitalization – when you start earning interest on your interest - is not capped in REPAYE (it is capped in PAYE). The interest you have not paid will be added back on top of the total loan amount at capitalization. So, your interest will capitalize if you refinance or switch programs.

Who should use REPAYE?

Because of the effective interest rate reduction, you can assume that REPAYE is the best program for you until proven otherwise. Whether you have a low income or a high debt burden, REPAYE is likely your best option.

Low income, average debt resident
Let's say that you are either single or married to someone who does not have an income. Maybe you couples matched, too. So, during your intern year, this is how your REPAYE payment would pan out: 10%

(AGI - 150% poverty line) = 10% (0 - some number) = zero.

So, your monthly payment is zero. Assuming you have $200,000 in debt at 6.5% interest, you are earning approximately $13,000 in annual interest, or $1,083 per month. Under REPAYE, the U.S. Department of Education would pay $541.50 on your loans each month, or $11,913 per year. Your effective interest rate would now be about 3.25% (compared to the 6.5% on the loans). This is called an effective interest rate reduction.

That's a great deal! And it's a much better deal than what you would get through private refinancing. This is why REPAYE is the assumed best program until proven otherwise.

High income, high debt resident
I want to drive home the point that personal finances are *personal*. Every person's situation is different. This is an example of how a high-income earner might still consider doing REPAYE if they have a huge debt burden.

Let's say that you are married to someone who makes $100,000 per year and that you earn $55,000 as a resident. For the poverty line assumption, let's say you live in the continental U.S. and that you have no children.

Here is how that payment works out:
10% (AGI - 150% Poverty Line) =
10% ($155,000-$24,690) = $13,031 annually.

If this high-income earning couple ($150,000 AGI) had $500,000 in debt, their monthly interest would be around $2,700. Following their monthly payment of $1,085, the rest is still up for the REPAYE subsidy.

So, the government would pay half of the remaining interest each month, or about $810. This would effectively reduce their interest rate from 6.5% to 4.5%. That's likely better than what they could get through a private refinance, which still leaves PSLF as an option on the table.

Who should avoid REPAYE?

Discussing who should avoid REPAYE is a bit more complicated. In general, if you are married to a high-income earner and do NOT have a boatload of debt (≥ $300,000), then REPAYE is probably not the best plan. The reason for this is evident in the following examples.

High income, average debt resident

Let's make the same assumptions as we did for the second group listed above who had a high income, but also had a high student loan debt burden. Here is how their REPAYE payment would shake out based on $150,000 AGI, no kids, and living in the continental U.S.:

10% (AGI - 150% Poverty Line) =
10% ($155,000-$24,690) = $13,031 annually.

Again, this comes out to a monthly payment of $1,085. So, unless they are gaining more than $1,000 in interest each month (i.e., have more than $200,000 in debt), they are not receiving an interest rate reduction through REPAYE. The government isn't paying for any of their interest, because their monthly payment already covered it all. As I ask my kids, "*good idea or bad idea?*" It's a bad idea if there is a better option. Honestly, this couple with a high income and low debt burden makes REPAYE's benefits null and void. Their best option is to probably refinance privately or to cap their interest using PAYE as discussed below.

Pay As You Earn (PAYE)

Before PAYE, the existing IBR and ICR programs weren't great: they offered little benefit and didn't qualify enough people. PAYE changed the ball game by offering some unique benefits. If REPAYE isn't right for you, you should consider PAYE.

Let's do this again in a pros and cons format.

Pros of PAYE

- PAYE caps your monthly payment at the Standard Repayment Plan (SRP) payment. Remember, REPAYE has no cap. This is why PAYE is better for high-income earning families. As your income increases, your payment eventually meets a ceiling: the SRP payment.
- PAYE caps the amount of interest that can capitalize at 10% of the original loan amount. So, if you have $200,000 in debt when you enter into PAYE, then only $20,000 can capitalize. If you've earned more interest, it will continue to grow but will never be added to the principle.

- PAYE has the same low monthly payment as REPAYE for low-income earners. It's still = 10% (AGI-150% poverty line).
- If you happen to have subsidized debt, PAYE will pay the interest on these for the first three years you are in the program.
- If you make 20 years' worth of monthly payments while enrolled in PAYE, your debt will be forgiven – though, unlike PSLF, the forgiven debt is taxed. This is better than the REPAYE taxed-forgiveness option, which requires 25 years of monthly payments.

Cons of PAYE

- PAYE does not pay a subsidy on unsubsidized debt. So, for medical school debt, there is no effective interest rate reduction if you received loans after 2012.
- It is harder to qualify for PAYE than it is to qualify for some of the other programs. You must be a new borrower after October 1st, 2007, and your direct loans (i.e., start of medical school) must have disbursed to you after October 11th, 2011. If you started medical school before October 2011, then you likely don't qualify.

Take Home

I realize this is a lot of information. As long as REPAYE makes sense for you (i.e., you are not high-income earning), you should use this program *even if you don't plan to pursue PSLF* because of the effective interest rate reduction. Once you have a contract in hand, privately refinance at the end of training and pay off the debt in 3-5 years by living like a resident.

If you plan on pursuing PSLF, then use REPAYE during training and a few months prior to graduation (while you still have a partial financial hardship), then switch to PAYE. This will cap your payments. After a year or two, you will no longer qualify for the partial financial hardship that is necessary for PAYE, and you will be enrolled in the standard repayment program. The goal throughout is to pay the lowest qualifying monthly payment for 120 months. We didn't make the game, we just get to play it.

If you've decided on PSLF because your debt-to-income ratio is too high ($\geq$ 1.5), then enroll in the best program you can, whatever that is. It just might be IBR if you don't qualify for REPAYE or PAYE.

For those of you who prefer flow charts, you read through all of that stuff above to get to this. The starting point here is for our fourth year medical students or interns. If you are past that point, just start with "Are you married?" Remember, if you have a massive student loan burden ($\geq$$300,000), sometimes REPAYE makes sense even if you are married to a high-income earner ($\geq$ $100,000 spousal income). Do the math.

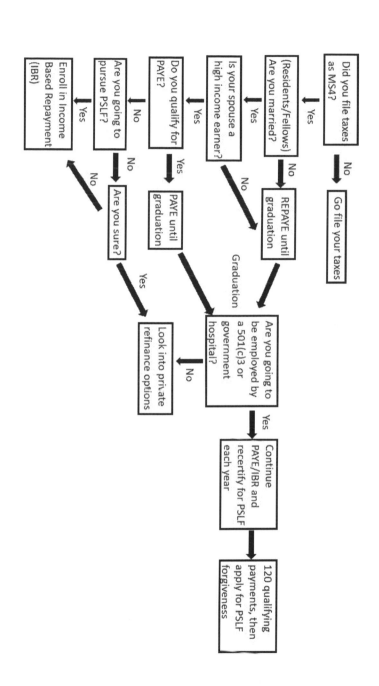

Did you file taxes as MS4?

→ Yes

No → Go file your taxes

(Residents/Fellows) Are you married?

→ Yes

No → REPAYE until graduation

Is your spouse a high income earner?

→ Yes

No → PAYE until graduation

Do you qualify for PAYE?

→ Yes → PAYE until graduation

No

Are you going to pursue PSLF?

Yes

No → Are you sure?

No

Yes → Look into private refinance options

Enroll in Income Based Repayment (IBR)

Graduation

Are you going to be employed by a 501(c)3 or government hospital?

No → Look into private refinance options

Yes → Continue PAYE/IBR and recertify for PSLF each year

→ 120 qualifying payments, then apply for PSLF forgiveness

85

Chapter 7:
Student Loan Debt
Management Part 2:
Private Student Loan
Refinancing Options

"Some debts are fun when you are acquiring them,
But none are fun when you set about retiring them."
~ Ogden Nash, unknown source

Remember my discussion at the beginning of this book about conflicts of interest. You should know that my website has a student loan refinancing page on it. If you choose to refinance through that page, I will receive money from that affiliate relationship. I view this as a conflict of interest. That said, if you decide to privately refinance your loans—which I would only encourage after careful thought and consideration— then do so wherever you find the best rate and the best kickback bonus. If that is not my website, please refinance through other sites! Also, if you skipped the last chapter assuming that PSLF just wasn't for you, then go read it. Remember,

REPAYE is usually the best repayment plan during training, even if you plan on privately refinancing later, because of the effective interest rate reduction.

Chapter 6 was written before chapter 7 for a reason. Once you privately refinance you cannot re-enter the federal landscape and go back into PSLF. Treat this like a cliff. Once you jump, there is no going back. You better have checked your parachute twice, done the calculation a few times, and determined the right course of action. I do not want anyone to regret the decision to privately refinance. Do your homework.

The algorithm found at the end of the previous chapter is pretty clear. While in training, REPAYE is superior to private refinancing most of the time. If you don't qualify for REPAYE or you are married to a high-income earner and do not qualify for PAYE, then you should consider whether you'll pursue PSLF or not. If you are absolutely certain PSLF isn't for you, then private refinancing during residency training is an option. Unfortunately, the redundancy here is necessary because this decision is that important.

With all of that said, this chapter is less complicated than the last one. We will discuss some useful information that everyone should know while in training and after. We will break this up into two sections 1) The basics on private refinancing and 2) Things that you need to consider when privately refinancing your loans.

The Basics

Resident refinancing programs allow you to privately refinance to a lower monthly payment with private companies at a rate that is often better than your current federal interest rate. That said, just because you can refinance as a resident doesn't mean you should. If you can get a better effective interest rate out of REPAYE than you can get out of privately refinancing, obviously REPAYE would be the better choice.

At the time of this writing, there are multiple private companies that will let you refinance during training. There is one other that will let you refinance once you have a contract in hand (i.e., you've signed on the dotted line for your first job out of training). Other companies will let you refinance earlier, but at a higher rate.

It's important to know that people can refinance more than once. The truth is, people can refinance as many times as they want. Consider refinancing at the beginning of residency (if REPAYE or PAYE isn't going to work out and you aren't pursuing PSLF), once you have a contract in hand, and then again about six months into your job when you have a better net worth. With each refinance, you'll likely receive a cash back bonus or rate reduction that you can put towards your loans, too.

When refinancing, always apply to multiple companies (at least three or four). The reason for this is to get the lowest interest rate for the desired term length (i.e. how many years you want to pay it back—7-year fixed, 10-year variable, etc.). Additionally, advertised rates on each company's website are exactly that, advertisements. The real rates are often different. Don't worry about credit score checks when you apply as all of these rates are "soft" checks on your credit and will not impact your credit score. Once you finally decide which one to pursue and apply you will undergo a "hard" credit check that actually matters. But this will only happen once you decide which company to use.

As for term lengths, shorter terms give you better rates, as does taking a variable rate over a fixed rate. I originally refinanced to a 7-year variable, but I paid off my $200,000 in loans in less than 2 years after finishing training. I probably should have taken a 5-year variable rate, but I didn't do that because I don't have personal disability insurance. I didn't want to "lock-in" a higher mandatory rate in case I became disabled. Many private refinancing companies provide language that allows you to take a break from payments if you should become disabled, but either way I wasn't taking the chance.

If you receive identical interest rates from multiple companies (for the same term length), then refinance with the company that best fits your interests. Consider the distinctions between various companies and choose based on that information.

How to Evaluate Refinancing Companies

There are some important differences between refinancing companies. It is your job to separate the wheat from the chaff. In order to do this, it is important to know what questions to ask. Rather than telling you what I think of each company as they are today, I want to teach you to do your own research. Here are the salient questions to ask:

1. What happens to your loans upon death or permanent disability? Where can you find this language? (You should ask to see it.) How

concrete is the language? Does it go to a board who decides if it will be forgiven or is it always discharged upon death?

2. Can you consolidate your loans with your spouse?   If you consolidate, what happens when one spouse dies? Does the spouse have to cosign? For example, I took on $40,000 of my wife's graduate school loans. I did not have her co-sign with me. If I die, her debt dies with me. She is a school teacher. There was no reason to leave her with a massive debt burden, though my term life insurance policy surely would have covered this anyway.

3. What kind of rates and term lengths do they supply? The shorter the repayment period, the lower the interest rate. Variable rates are often lower than fixed. Take the shortest variable rate you are comfortable with taking. The interest rate would have to go up immediately after refinancing and go up *a lot* for you to lose money compared to a fixed loan. Do what's right for you, though; you have to pick terms that allow you to sleep at night.

4. Speaking of disability, you should ask what happens to your loans in times of hardship (permanent disability, loss of job, etc.). Not all companies treat this the same. Ask for the specific language from their policy.

5. Is there a maximum amount that the company will refinance? Some companies can refinance a greater loan amount than others.

6. Do they contribute to a social cause you care about? Some companies give to social causes

when you refinance through them. The company I chose sponsors a child's education in a different country with each loan that they refinance.

Take Home

Here comes the bullet point take away:
- Refinancing options exist for both residents and attendings.
- Only pursue refinancing once you are *certain* that you are not interested in pursuing PSLF.
- Make sure you apply to multiple companies and get multiple rates.
- Ask the tough questions to separate the companies and find the one that is best for your situation.

Chapter 8:
Personal Finance During Residency

"It's supposed to be hard. If it wasn't hard, everyone would do it.
The hard … is what makes it great."
~ Jimmy Dugan (in *A League of Their Own*)

This chapter may seem a little early and incomplete; it's because we are following a chronological timeline in this book. The Full Monty on investing and asset protection comes later. The truth is that most residents can only afford to invest a small amount of money during training, and they only need so much insurance. Here we will focus on what a resident needs to consider in terms of personal finance, so that you can focus on your real job—learning your craft and becoming a great attending physician.

Asset Protection

When I finished medical school, my net worth was south of negative $200,000. You might wonder, "*What assets did he have to protect?*" As a resident, your net worth may be very negative. But your net worth isn't your biggest asset. Your most important asset is you and your human capital, or earning potential. You need to protect both of those assets.

Term life insurance

If you are married or have kids, then you probably need term life insurance. As a resident, how much you need depends on your financial picture. To come up with a reasonable number, add up the following and round the numbers to the closest $50,000 increment:

- Cost of any liabilities/debts you may have (cars, house, refinanced student loans, etc.).
- Cost of your entire salary you would earn during residency so that your spouse is not forced to work (e.g., $55,000 per year for 5-year residency = $275,000). If your spouse has an earned-income you may adjust this number accordingly.
- Cost of education for any kids you have ($200,000 per kid).

What this looked like for me in residency was the following: House ($120,000) + one financed car ($30,000) + student loans ($200,000) + 4-year anesthesia residency ($220,000) + one kid at the time for college ($200,000) = $770,000. So, my wife and I each took out a $750,000 term-life insurance policy during residency. It cost us about $50-100 per month.

The kind of insurance that you want is term life insurance with a level premium (i.e., you pay a set premium for the duration of the policy). Notice that **I did not say whole life insurance**, cash value insurance, or any other insurance product that mixes investments and insurance. These are not the ideal product for the vast majority of people out there, no matter how good an insurance salesperson makes them sound!

When you finish training, you will need to increase your term life insurance to better suit your new earning potential.

Disability insurance

The other asset you need to protect is your income earning potential in the case that you become disabled. The piece of mind a disability insurance policy provides cannot be overemphasized. Trust me, I know what it's like not to be able to have that peace of mind. An insurance salesman destroyed any chances I had of getting personal disability insurance when I was a fourth-year medical student.   Don't make the same mistake.

If you have any medical problems at all, wait until you become an intern and then get your hospital's version of the "guaranteed" disability insurance policy for residents. Typically, the only requirement is that you cannot have been previously declined for disability insurance. Since you knew better and never applied, this won't be an issue. Once you have the guaranteed policy in hand, then you can feel free to take a look at less expensive policies offered by other insurance companies where a medical exam is required. If you get denied at this juncture, then it's no loss to you because you have a guaranteed policy in hand. If you get accepted, then you've earned the right to purchase a less expensive policy to cover you if you become disabled and can now get rid of the guaranteed policy you no longer need.

You should purchase your disability insurance from an independent agent (not tied to a specific company) who has extensive experience working with physicians. Your policy should include the following:
- ❑ Specialty - and occupation - specific disability definition: You don't want to be forced to

perform a different kind of medicine if disability restricts you from practicing your specialty.

- ❑ Only six companies currently offer a true own-occupation definition: Berkshire Life (a Guardian Company), Ohio National, Principal, Standard Insurance Company, Ameritas, and MassMutual.
- ❑ Future purchase option: You want the option to increase your coverage in the future without having to undergo future medical exams. This is particularly important for residents who cannot afford what they will need as an attending, but want the option to buy it later.
- ❑ Residual disability rider: This rider provides benefits in the case of partial disability.
- ❑ Inflation protection: This feature means your potential benefit will grow along with inflation.

Different Groups Have Different Goals

Now that we have covered asset protection, let's talk investing. When it comes to investing during residency, there is no one-size-fits-all answer. Each resident's situation is unique. Our goal is to help the majority make good choices. For this purpose, I think residents generally fit into three distinct groups:

Group 1: The resident with debt who is pursuing PSLF

Approximately 80% of residents come out of medical school with debt. The median debt burden is just under $200,000. Hopefully, after reading the two preceding chapters, you now have a plan to attack your debt.

If you are pursuing PSLF, recognize that the goal is to pay the minimum required qualifying payment, to certify in a qualifying program every year, and to have as much debt as possible forgiven after you complete 120 payments. (*For the moral pundits out there: don't hate the player, hate the game.*) Because you are making minimum payments, you should have some money to invest if you are budgeting properly.

Group 2: The resident in debt who is NOT pursuing PSLF

If you are not pursuing PSLF, then your goal is to minimize the total amount of debt burden that must be paid back. As was discussed previously, if you are single or married to a low- or no-income earner, this is usually accomplished via REPAYE during residency. If you do not qualify for REPAYE, this may be accomplished through private refinancing.

The next question is whether you should pay down your debt or invest. We discuss the thought process involved in answering that question in chapter 11. During training, you'll probably get more bang for your buck by paying off your debt (and keeping interest from accruing/capitalizing) than you will from investing. That said, if you are enrolled in REPAYE you need to see if additional money paid over the minimum is applied to the principle or if it will decrease your subsidy.

For this group, I am definitely of the mindset that you should take the guaranteed return on your money by paying down your debt instead of investing. If you can get a guaranteed 6% (that won't add to your debt), why put money in the market and "hope" it works out better than that? Pay off the debt. That said, everyone's situation is different and your job is to make intentional decisions with the right information.

Group 3: The resident with no debt

What if you are in the 20% of graduates who do not have medical school debt? Well, first off, congratulations are in order. You've been given a head start, which is great news. Your job now? Don't screw it up! I wish I were kidding, but the truth is that residents are prone to consumer debt. Just don't do it. There is one great way to prevent that problem, and we discussed it earlier: budgeting.

Behavioral finance matters and you should learn to save now during residency. Your income may seem small, but you make as much as the median income in our country. Don't make excuses. Aim to save 20% of your AGI.

Why Should You Invest During Residency?

If you are in group 1 or group 3, you may be asking, "*Why should I invest during residency?*" There are a lot of reasons, but let me highlight the salient ones before we talk about where to put your money.

Reason 1: It will matter in the end (do the math).

Let's make some assumptions and look at the math: You have a four-year residency and save $5,500 in a Roth IRA each year. Assuming 6% interest growth over those four years, you will have saved $24,952 at the end of residency. (Remember, when you take money out at retirement there are a lot of reasons why you want to save your Roth money for last.)

How much will that $24,952 saved during residency be worth at the end of retirement 50 years later (25 year career + 25 years into retirement)? The figure below illustrates the growth. The short answer is that the $24,952 you invested during residency will grow to more than $370,000 (assuming 7% growth on that money). If you are married and max out your spouse's Roth IRA too, you can double that to $740,000. I don't know many people who would say that $740,000 isn't worth it.

Also, know that there is a limited amount of Roth space each year ($6,000 per individual in 2019). If you don't put money into your IRA for that year, you lose the opportunity to do so until the next year. For the residents saying, "*I'll just contribute to that space when I am an attending*" you must realize this isn't an option. That Roth space is just left unfilled. Forever.

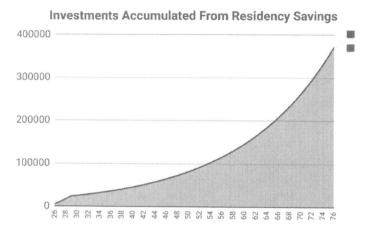

Figure 1. Investments from residency contributions: Age (years) on
x-axis; investment ($) totals on y-axis

Reason 2: There are tax benefits for you.

The first tax benefit is straightforward. When you invest
pre-tax dollars in a 403B/401K at work, your AGI will
decrease and you'll owe less taxes. This can also
lower your payments if enrolled in an IDR program.
However, many residency programs do not match
(e.g., your employer places $1 into your retirement
account with each $1 you contribute), which is why I
think it's smart to put money into a Roth IRA instead. If
you are lucky enough to have a match at your training
program, take advantage of it! Otherwise, you are
leaving part of your salary on the table.

The second (lesser known) tax benefit to investing in
residency is that some residents may be able to receive
a Retirement Savings Contributions Credit (see the
chart below, which is taken directly from the IRS
website). While this won't apply to high-income

earning residency couples, it does apply to some other married residents. If you are single, skip to the next section.

This tax credit is limited to a $4,000 maximum, if married. The percentage of your IRA contribution that you get to take as a credit depends on whether you are single or married and on your gross income. Resident couples who earn less than $63,000 are eligible for a 10% credit on your $6,000 IRA contribution. In other words, you'll get a dollar-for-dollar decrease of $600 off your tax bill when you file (all because you invested in an IRA).

Note that this tax credit does not apply to full-time students. So, to my medical student friends reading this a bit early, don't fall into that trap. (Consider this again when you get to residency; your job in medical school is to minimize debt!)

2018 Saver's Credit

Credit Rate	Married Filing Jointly	Head of Household	All Other Filers*
50% of your contribution	AGI not more than $38,000	AGI not more than $28,500	AGI not more than $19,000
20% of your contribution	$38,001 - $41,000	$28,501 - $30,750	$19,001 - $20,500
10% of your contribution	$41,001 - $63,000	$30,751 - $47,250	$20,501 - $31,500
0% of your contribution	more than $63,000	more than $47,250	more than $31,500

Source: https://www.irs.gov/retirement-plans/plan-participant-employee/retirement-savings-contributions-savers-credit

Reason 3: Investing will help you learn behavioral finance.

Perhaps the biggest reason to invest during training is because it teaches vital behavioral finance lessons. It teaches you to save a percentage of your AGI each year. This will make it easy to continue to save when your income increases. At that point, you will have trained yourself that saving a percentage of your income is *just what you do*. It'll be in your financial DNA. Saving a portion of your income will also teach one other important lesson: the art of paying your future self first and your current self last.

The Practical Guide to Investing in Residency

Now that you are properly convinced of the merits of investing during training, it's now my responsibility to tell you how to do it. Here is a basic primer on investing based on the Pareto Principle (all that you need to know). For finer details on investing, please read chapter 11. As a resident, assuming that you have no access to other income, this chapter is likely all you need to know.

Investing philosophy

Before we get to it, you should know that I believe in passive or index fund investing. Whether index funds are better than actively managed funds is an academic question. The jury is out and the question has been adequately answered.[14] Unless you have a very good reason not to invest in index funds (i.e. they aren't offered at your institution), this is the way to go. Benefits of index fund investing include: lower costs granted through lower expense ratios, decreased transaction costs, and the ability to simply mirror the market with a diversified portfolio. Time in the market, or how long your money has the opportunity experience the magic of compounding interest, will ultimately be the key to success.

Not only are index funds better, but they also remove the need to constantly check your investments. The goal is to simply match the market. No better, no worse. There is no need to waste time trying to beat the market, time the market (i.e. guess when the market is going up or down), or to try to pick the winning stock. It has been shown that the more often you check your portfolio, the more likely you are to change something (which usually hurts more than it helps).[15] Just set it and forget it.

The "set it and forget it" method of investing I recommend is exactly what I do with my own finances. As a resident, with arguably less time, this "set it and

[14] SPIVA Scorecard. https://www.spglobal.com/en/research-insights/articles/SPIVA-US-Scorecard . Accessed January 25th, 2019.

[15] Thaler RH, Tversky A, Khaneman D, and Scwartz A. *The Effect of Myopia and Loss Aversion on Risk Taking: An Experimental Test*. The Quarterly Journal of Economics, Volume 112, Issue 2, 1 May 1997, Pages 647–661. https://doi.org/10.1162/003355397555226 Accessed January 25th, 2019.

forget it" mentality is even more important. Don't waste your time speculating on cryptocurrency or tulip bulbs (put "tulip bulb craze" into your search engine if you don't know about it). Focus your time on learning your craft and becoming the best physician you can be. If you don't believe me and need a comprehensive book to change your mind about index fund investing, then go read *A Random Walk on Wall Street* by Burton G. Malkiel.

What? You don't have time to do that? Then, just invest in index funds. You can thank me later by telling your friends to buy this book.

Asset allocation

Asset allocation is the percentage of your retirement portfolio that you've chosen to allocate, or place, into various investment securities, such as stocks, bonds, or specific kinds of funds. Choosing your asset allocation for your Roth IRA does not have to be complicated. Just choose a total stock market index fund at your favorite company and put the vast majority (75-90%) of your money in there. Put the remaining percentage (10-25%) in a total bond index fund. This is a best practice because the total stock market index fund buys the whole American stock market and the total bond index fund does the same for bonds. Diversification in the market is key to mitigate risk. Total stock market funds do just that. The companies that are known for offering these are Vanguard, Fidelity, and Charles Schwab. I prefer Vanguard, because the founder of Vanguard, John "Jack" Bogle (1929 – 2019) , started the first index fund and Vanguard is the only mutual fund company owned by the stockholders (i.e., their main goal is to maximize your earnings). However, you can sometimes find lower cost expense ratios – the cost to you, the shareholder, for managing the fund – in funds at the other two companies.

If your employer offers you a retirement account as a resident and you have additional money to invest above the $6,000 IRA contribution ($12,000 if married), then feel free to put it into your 401K/403B. Where should you put it? This may be more complicated, because you may not have the choice of a total stock market index fund in a 403B/401K. You still want diversification, though. If your plan doesn't offer total market index funds, pick something that makes sense. You can refer to chapter 11 for examples.

The best way to make contributions

Rather than make one lump sum contribution into your IRA, as a resident, you can simply dollar cost average (DCA) your way through the year. Dollar cost averaging means to place a fixed amount of money into a retirement vehicle on regular basis. This means investing a small portion of each paycheck into the vehicle of your choice consistently each month. This is better than keeping your money out of the market for the entire year until you have the money saved up. Otherwise, you will potentially be missing out on compounding interest.

If you are investing $6,000 for the year, divide that by 12 and you need to transfer $500 from your paycheck – if paid monthly – into your Roth IRA each month. Just set it up on auto-draft. It should be part of your budget.

Note: Direct contributions to a Roth IRA are allowed until your AGI exceeds $122,000 (single) or $193,000 (married) according to 2019 IRS rules. After this, the "phase out" begins, which limits the amount you can place directly into a Roth IRA. Because residents - unlike attending physicians earning >$122,000 (single) – typically don't have to worry about an income of this size, they can dollar cost average into a Roth IRA. This does NOT apply when you start a Backdoor Roth IRA as an attending. You should not dollar cost average into a backdoor Roth IRA if you are earning more than $122,000 (single). More on that in chapter 11.

Take Home

Hopefully, this chapter has highlighted the importance of investing while in training. For those who like the highlights, here they are:

- If you are in PSLF or have no debt, you should be investing during residency. It will matter in the end.
- If you have refinanced debt, just put any extra money into that. (I should mention that this is a personal decision and others may say to put money into the market.)
- If you are investing, see if your employer has a 403B/401K match. If so, contribute enough to get the match.
- If no match is available, then prefer a Roth IRA instead.
- If available, put 75-90% of the money into a total stock market index fund and 10-25% into a total bond index fund. Determine the amount placed in each based on your risk tolerance.

- If those options aren't available, try to mirror it as much as possible utilizing the index funds offered by your employer.
- Auto draft your money each month for your investments.
- Just forget about it until the end of residency (you could rebalance each year, but it probably won't matter much).

After that, focus on your real job which is to be the best resident physician you can be. Ask tough questions. Make decisions on your own before you ask the attending. Then, ask and see if you were right or not. Demand autonomy. Finally, remember to read, read, read.

Chapter 9:
Live Like a Resident
(AFTER Residency)

"Whatever your income, always live below your means."
~ Thomas J. Stanley, *The Millionaire Next Door*

We have already covered a lot. Despite that, this is probably the most important chapter. Nothing sets you on a trajectory for early financial independence, or a career in debt, more than what you do in that first two years after you finish training.

To my knowledge, it was Dr. Jim Dahle who made the phrase "live like a resident" famous in his book *The White Coat Investor: A Doctor's Guide to Personal Finance and Investing*. If you haven't read it, you should. I buy a copy for all of my resident advisees.

Dr. Dahle says it this way:

"The most important year in a physician's life is [their] first year out of training, and the most important advice this book can give you is contained in just four words. ***Live Like A Resident!"***

When you're right, you're right. In my first year of being an attending anesthesiologist I increased my net worth (assets - debts) by more than $250,000 while paying off $128,000 in student loan debt and accruing $150,000 in assets through investments. How did I do that in just one year? By living like a resident. And, somehow, I was still able to do some things that I really enjoyed (like going on a Disney cruise, buying a car, and getting a country club membership).

We will answer one of the more common questions in the next chapter ("Should I invest or pay down debt?"). This chapter is going to really hammer home why it is so important to live within your means once you finish. At the end of the chapter, I'll show you the rule I use to accomplish all of our financial goals while still allowing for some life improvement after training. Before we discuss that, I want to spend some time outlining why living like a resident early on is so important.

The $2 Million Thought Experiment

Initially, your savings rate is the main determinant of your success in investing. Your money will start to work for you once you've saved a substantial amount. Why is this initial savings rate so important right after you finish? Let's perform an experiment to illustrate the point.

Your goal in this thought experiment is to get to $2 million, which would provide roughly $80,000 of income in retirement. Here are the assumptions. You save $50,000 every year and earn 8% in interest annually. Given these assumptions, it would take you 19 years to get to that goal (you'd actually be sitting at $2,072,313 at the end of year 19).

After ten years of savings making $50,000 in annual contributions, you will have around $700,000. Of this, $500,000 comes from your contributions ($50,000 x 10 years), which accounts for ~70% of the entire total of your accumulated savings ($500,000 out of the $700,000). Why should you care? Well, this proves that the major determinant in building wealth early on is your savings rate, or contributions. The interest earned on your money has not made a substantial impact yet.

After you have built a critical mass of savings, the second decade looks very different! After 17 years you will find the break even point. This is the point at which your total savings has more to do with accrued compound interest than your annual contributions. Up until this point, the amount you have contributed matters more than the interest you have gained. The point is this – the longer you delay building wealth, the longer it takes for your money to work. You don't want to spend your whole life working for money. You want your money to work for you.

The Big Five

Now that you know that saving early on is vital to success, let's discuss expenses that can prevent you from being able to save. The more money you spend, the less money you can save. As we previously discussed, the purpose of making a budget is to free up money so that you can accomplish your financial goals. If you are spending too much, then you won't have any money left to build wealth.

Traditionally, the "big three" expenses are housing, transportation (cars), and food. I'd also add in childcare (or private school) and vacations. If people get these five categories right in the first few years after training, they'll likely have enough money left over to accomplish their goals. If, however, they decide to fulfill all of that delayed gratification from their long training period, they will be in a bad spot. When someone buys the big house and the mortgage payment eats up a ton of their monthly paycheck, guess what? There is no money left to be put towards that savings rate. Ever heard of being "house poor"?

The point I am trying to make here is that people who have really nice things are often not wealthy. Unless everything you own is paid off, wealth has nothing to do with the house in which you live, the car you drive, or the fancy food you eat. It has to do with assets and debts. Someone panhandling on the corner of the street likely has a higher net worth than the 80% of residents who are graduating with debt. Would you think it reasonable for the panhandler to buy a $750,000 home or to finance a $70,000 car? That probably means you shouldn't either.

Let's consider an example. If you buy a $750,000 house, your mortgage (assuming 30-year fixed at 4% interest) will cost you $5,000 per month. If you instead chose to live in a more affordable place that cost $1,000 per month for just two years, you would have an extra $48,000 to put towards your student loans or retirement each year. Living like a resident for a couple of extra years will set you up for success. The big house, nice car, fancy food, private school, and expensive vacations can wait until you can afford them.

Introduction to the 10% Rule

As you'll find out in the last chapter, I am a big advocate of balance. Yes, doctors need to sit down and create a budget or track their spending. Doctors also need to save a lot of money in whatever way they can. That said, it's also important to live a little. None of us are promised tomorrow. The question is, how much fun do we have?

Well, that's what the following rule is all about. It's a gauge, or a barometer, for making the tough decision of how much to enjoy versus how much to save. I follow this rule pretty strictly, and used it to increase our net worth by over $250,000 in one year. As long as you follow the principle being taught by the rule, financial success will not be far behind.

The 10% Rule

When you finish training, your take home pay will increase by $5,000-$20,000 per month. Maybe more for some specialists. Regardless, it's a substantial increase in pay. It's very easy to see that money enter your bank account, to remember the sacrifices made over the last seven to ten years, and to spend every nickel and dime of that huge paycheck. Don't think you could spend it all? Go look at all of those NFL and NBA players who were given sizeable amounts of money and are now broke or bankrupt. Americans are consumers. It's one of our national pastimes.

There are multiple times in life where you receive a bump in pay. It may be due to a large (or small) promotion, like the one you experience right after finishing training. It may be a quarterly or annual bonus.

It may be because you achieved an incentivized milestone, such as an academic or clinically-related incentive. Maybe you receive an inheritance of some kind. The 10% Rule should be applied in any situation where you receive an increase in the amount you take home.

The 10% Rule: For every increase in pay or bonus that you receive, take 10% of that money and spend it on whatever your heart desires (fancy food, stuff, entertainment, etc.). Put the other 90% towards wealth accumulation (paying down debt or investing).

For example, when my family's take home pay went from $5,000 per month in my (non-accredited) regional anesthesia fellowship to making $15,000 as an attending physician, I took 10% of this raise (or $1,000) and I applied this money towards lifestyle creep. The 10% Rule allows us to give 10% to the heart while we apply the other 90% towards wise financial decisions (destroying debt, investing in passive low-cost funds, starting a backdoor Roth IRA, saving for your kids' 529s, etc).

So, how did I spend my 10%? Well, I spent it on the one thing that every financially minded person tells you not to spend your money on … I financed a car. The year I finished training was the last year the car I financed was being made. While I am not a huge believer in financing cars, I couldn't have taken it home any other way. To make myself feel better, I should say that this isn't just any car; it's a Chevrolet SS. A four-door sedan with naturally aspirated V8, which produces 415 horse-power and is controlled with a 6-speed manual transmission. Oh, and it can fit three car seats in the back ("Daddy go faster!").

I am not done yet, though. The car payment costs us about $650 per month. According to the 10% rule, I still had another $350 to spend, and so my wife and I bought a monthly membership to a country club, which gave us access to a swimming pool, two golf courses, six tennis courts, a driving range, and the clubhouse for food.

Have I committed personal finance blasphemy? Well, since I was following the 10% Rule, I recognized that I was still going to reach my financial goals. Using the other 90%, we increased our net worth by over $250,000 in one year. We crushed $128,000 in student loans in 12 months, and saved $150,000 in assets through our retirement accounts. All in all, the vast majority of my take home pay from monthly paychecks and bonuses continues to go towards building wealth. If I am being honest, once all of our debt is gone (except our mortgage), this may turn into the 20% rule. Until that point, 10% has been more than enough to really feel like we are enjoying the pay increase after residency while still accomplishing all of our financial goals, too.

Take Home

The early years after you finish training are the most important. You either set yourself up on a trajectory for success or you set yourself up on a painful path of indebtedness. Use the 10% Rule to understand that you can "live a little" when you finish while still using the vast majority of your money to get started on the right foot by building wealth. To drive home some of these points, the next chapter will discuss the divergent paths that two doctors take (one towards wealth, and the other towards spending). Which path will you choose?

Chapter 10:
A Tale of Two Doctors

"I shall be telling this with a sigh
Somewhere ages and ages hence:
Two roads diverged in a wood and I -
I took the one less traveled by,
and that has made all the difference."
~ Robert Frost, *The Road Not Taken*

The pastor that married my wife and me often said, *"You can never hear true things enough."* The point he was trying to make was that if someone tells you something valuable (even if you have already heard it, you should listen again). Having reminders in life that point us in the right direction can only be a good thing. This chapter is no different.

Living like a resident after training is so important that I didn't want to stop with the prior chapter. You really can never hear this stuff enough. Living like a resident is likely the single most important determining factor of your ability to build wealth quickly and to obtain financial independence, possibly ever. That said, I also want you to see, in a real example, that you can use the 10% Rule to bump your lifestyle a bit and still achieve your important goals.

Let's compare the example of two doctors and the decisions that they make. Follow along as we determine their ultimate trajectory. Will you take the road less traveled to early financial independence? Or will you allow decisions to ensnare you in debt? Let this tale of two doctors help you make that decision.

The Assumptions for the Two Doctors

The biggest problem when you earn your first "real" paycheck is that many of the choices you make are often binding. You cannot easily reverse a lot of decisions. For example, if you buy a million-dollar home with nothing down through a physician home loan and then find you want or need to sell it a year later, you better believe that financial pain will be real. Expect to pony up $100,000-$120,000 to sell that house. Six percent of the closing cost will go to the realtors. The other four percent will go to origination fees, closing, and the mortgage banker/broker.

The set-up

We will follow Dr. Jones and Dr. EFI (Early Financial Independence) as they make very different choices when they finish training. We will discuss each doctor's lifestyle inflation after training, decisions about student loans, retirement planning, and eventual trajectory.

Let's make some assumptions for both of them, though:

- Both doctors are 35 years old when they finish training.
- They are both married, and their spouses do not work.
- Both doctors have $250,000 in debt.
- They each have a starting annual salary of $250,000.
- They both made the smart decision to get term life insurance and disability insurance.

- They both privately refinanced their loans.

Introducing Dr. Jones

Dr. Jones has waited long enough. She spent four years in undergrad, four years in medical school, four years in anesthesiology residency, a year in fellowship, and now she is ready to reap the rewards of a lot of hard work. She wants to live the doctor's life.

She doesn't want to keep up with the Dr. Joneses. She *is* Dr. Jones.

Lifestyle changes after residency

Her monthly take home paycheck is now $14,500. That's more than $10,000 larger than her last residency paycheck! After signing her new contract, she found the exact house that she wants. It's only $800,000 with a 4% interest rate. With a 30-year fixed mortgage that makes for a monthly payment of $4,100.

And the garage will fit the two new BMWs she bought for herself and her spouse perfectly. She got a steal with 3.5% financing for a monthly payment of $1,800 to cover both cars. Don't forget the $200 monthly car insurance payment.

She understands that she could pay down her debt quickly or max out her 401K and take advantage of her employer's voluntary match, but she just doesn't see the need for that right now. Retirement is 30 years away. Her employer has a mandatory contribution, so she puts in the required 2% match ($5,000 per year), but doesn't see a lot of other reasons to save for retirement. She doesn't even know what a backdoor Roth is because saving for retirement couldn't be further from her current plans. It's just too far away.

As for her student loans, she knows that she doesn't want to keep her loans around forever. So, she refinanced. Her $250,000 in student loans are now being paid via a 10-year fixed plan with a 3.5% interest rate. The monthly payment on this will be around $2,500.

Here is how her monthly paycheck would break down.

$14,500 take home pay
-$4,100 mortgage payment
-$2,000 car payment and insurance
-$2,500 student loan payment
-$300 disability and life insurance
$5,600 remaining

This leaves Dr. Jones and her spouse with $5,600 for all of their other living expenses. These might include a country club membership, mobile phones, designer clothes/jewelry, cable TV, premium gas for the BMWs, eating out, vacations, utilities, etc. She also hasn't even put furniture in the house she just bought. But that can probably just go on a credit card, right? All of her bonus pay will go into the awesome vacations she and her spouse deserve. They're working hard!

The next thirty years

The take home here is that Dr. Jones is living large. Because she bought the house and the cars, and she is not being aggressive with her student loans, she is really going to get behind the eight ball. How far behind? Let's see.

Given Dr. Jones's lifestyle, she would probably want to have $200,000 each year in retirement. According to The 4% Rule – which we will discuss in chapter 12 – in order to retire she would likely need $200,000 x 25 = $5,000,000. If her current plan continues, and we assume an 8% interest growth on the $10,000 ($5,000 x 2 for her employer match) she is saving each year. After ten years (age 45), she will have an unimpressive $161,000 saved for retirement. At that point her debt would be gone. Maybe I am not giving her plan enough credit. What if she started saving after that point?

Let's say she starts maxing out her 401K and with her employer's contribution and additional voluntary matching, she invests $57,000 (the maximum allowed for 401Ks in 2019) for the next 20 years. Assuming 8% growth, how much will she have at age 65? The answer is a little more than $2.8 million. Taking 4% of that each year for retirement, she would have $112,000 per year.

Remember, because of her lifestyle, she needed $200,000 per year. So, that's half of what she wanted for retirement and she is now 65. Unless things change drastically for her, she will likely never get to that goal. This is a story of taking a big lifestyle inflation after you finish training, which leads to a low savings rate. Just don't do it. Unless you never want to retire at your current lifestyle.

Introducing Dr. EFI

Fortunately, there are better examples and Dr. Early Financial Independence (Dr. "EFI") is going to show you that. Dr. EFI knows better. She has completed her four years of medical school, four years of anesthesiology residency, and also did a one-year fellowship. She wants to start off on the right foot. She has done her homework and knows enough about personal finance to do it herself.

With a more moderate approach to the lifestyle bump after residency, Dr. EFI is not going to chase after a house three times her income. She is going to buy a great house someday. Just not right now. Before she buys the house, she is going to make some good financial decisions. She will still enjoy a bump in lifestyle after finishing training, but Dr. EFI is going to keep that lifestyle bump in check. Let's see how she does compared to Dr. Jones.

Lifestyle changes after residency

Because she maxes out her 401K (pre-tax $19,000). Dr. EFI's take home pay is $13,700 utilizing the same federal and state tax assumptions as Dr. Jones. Dr. EFI followed the 10% Rule when she saw her paycheck increase dramatically. She took about 10% of that increase and decided to bump her lifestyle. She has earned that.

She moves into a small rental home for $1,000 per month. It's slightly bigger than the $750 apartment they were staying in during her fellowship year. She drove a beater during her years in medical school and residency to keep costs as low as she could. But she really likes the new Toyota Prius (Touring edition for $30,000) because it gets almost 60 miles per gallon. Making the same assumption as we did for Dr. Jones, she decides to surprise her spouse with one, too.

Despite the advice from other personal finance blogs and books, she finances a car. At 3.5% for five years, this will cost her approximately $1,000 per month for both cars, including insurance. Dr. EFI wants to keep this plan in place for three years after she finishes. Once her student loans are gone, she will be able to finally reap the real rewards. How can she have so much discipline? Well, she realizes that her lifestyle is going to be a little better with these changes, and— more importantly—she understands how important these beginning years are to her financial success.

Dr. EFI decides to max out her 401K to take advantage of her employer's 2% required match, 4% voluntary match, and employer contribution. With everything included, she is maxed out to the 401K limit of $56,000. Dr. EFI's take home pay is $800 less than Dr. Jones' each month ($9,600 less for the year), but because of her employer match, she is saving $52,000 more each year than Dr. Jones. You read that right: she is only contributing $13,000 more than Dr. Jones, but she saves an extra $51,000 by contributing $13,000 more. That's a steal right there.

Dr. EFI and her spouse also max out the $12,000 each year for their backdoor Roth ($6,000 annual maximum per spouse in 2019). In all, she is investing $68,000 by contributing $31,000 of her own money. After her student loans are paid off, she will apply the 10% Rule again and have even more going towards investments, likely in a taxable account.

Dr. EFI wants to be done with her student loans as quickly as possible. So, she refinanced her loans to a 5-year variable because she knew this would offer her the best rate. We will say she averages 3.25% interest and she decides to pay $6,000 per month in student loans. This way, her loans will be gone in 3.5 years with no additional payments. If she takes any extra bonus money she receives and, according to the 10% Rule, puts the other 90% of her bonus pay towards her loans; her loans would likely be gone in less than three years.

What will Dr. EFI do differently after her student loans (which have been costing her $6,000 per month) are paid off? She plans to combine about a third of that money ($2,000) with her current home rental payment ($1,000) and putting that total ($3,000) towards a mortgage on a new "doctor" house ($3,000 mortgage payment on a $550,000 home)[16]. She put another $3,000 into a taxable account. That additional $36,000 per year will take her annual investments to $104,000.

We have accounted for $5,000 of the previous $6,000 monthly student loan payment. What about the remaining $1,000 per month? That, my friend, is for pure enjoyment on whatever she wants to spend it on. She could put it towards her mortgage and pay it off in 20 years instead of 30. Or she could take two $6,000 vacations each year. It's up to her and her spouse.

---

[16] This home price is not representative of all markets, and the author recognizes that homes may cost more than this in areas with higher cost of living.

We saw the breakdown of Dr. Jones's paycheck above. Dr. EFI is saving much more and has had a small amount of lifestyle inflation. Here is how Dr. EFI's monthly paycheck looks under the same assumptions (state and federal taxes) as Dr. Jones (which is listed to the side for comparison):

	Dr. EFI	Dr. Jones
Take home pay	$13,700	$14,500
House/apartment payment	~$1,000	~$4,100
Car payment + insurance	~$1,000	~$2,000
Student loan payment	~$6,000	~$2,500
Backdoor Roth (post-tax) IRA money	~$1,000	$0
Disability and life insurance	~$300	~$300
Remaining money	$4,400 remaining	$5,600 remaining

Dr. EFI has $4,400 (post-tax) to spend each month; Dr. Jones has $5,600. But Dr. EFI's $4,400 is definitely more than she had as a resident or fellow. Despite financing two new cars and living in a slightly better place than in residency, she still has more spending money than she did as a resident—for eating out, going to the movies, or catching a ball game.

The next ten (and thirty) years

What does she get for the $1,200 sacrifice she is making each month compared to Dr. Jones? **Ten years out** from training she will be able to accomplish the following:

- Student loans paid off in three years (compared to 10 years and a lot of extra interest paid by Dr. Jones)
- She will have accumulated over $1,286,000 in her investment accounts (compared to the ~$161,000 of Dr. Jones)
- She will have a very positive net worth (compared to Dr. Jones' very negative net worth)
- She will be well on her way to financial independence (Dr. Jones will never be able to retire at her current lifestyle)

Dr. EFI is making some real progress! She and her spouse determine that once all of their debt is gone (no more car loans, mortgage, and college for kids if they have any) they could live very comfortably on $120,000 per year in retirement. They understand the power of a relatively "frugal" life. Since they want to retire early they need it to last a little longer. So, they multiply their desired annual number by 30 (instead of 25 for traditional retirement mandated by The 4% Rule). They will need $120,000 x 30 = $3,000,000 to retire. If they take out 4% ($120,000 per year), that should last as long as they need it.

If she doesn't change anything about her investments above, Dr. EFI will have her $3 million by age 52. If she were to increase her investments in her taxable account by $1,000 per month (say, when those first cars are paid off after five years), she would reach that goal a year earlier at age 51. Not too bad! Being able to retiring at age 51, or practice medicine because she wants to, would be swell. That's only 16 years after she finished training.

This is all assuming no increase in pay, no additional money from bonuses towards investments (which she would obviously make), and that her spouse never works or has retirement accounts of their own. If any of those things happened, they would likely meet their goals in their mid - to late - 40s. This is only 10 to 15 years after she finished training. When Dr. EFI reaches financial independence, she could choose to be a doctor and work because she wants to, but she would not working because she has to for financial reasons. That's the power of wise choices and the 10% Rule.

All the while, Dr. Jones will still be unable to retire at age 65 (15 years after Dr. EFI can). And that's even if she really turned it around after a decade of making mistakes. Yikes. Compounding interest is wonderful, but it takes time! That's why your decisions early on are so important.

Take Home

I should mention that there is a middle ground where you save 20% of your AGI each year and comfortably retire at 60 or 65. But you can also get there much sooner, if you want. Who knows how much you will love your job in 20 years?

You can have an increase in lifestyle immediately after you finish training, but you have to keep it in check. You can have most anything (except the huge house), but you can't have everything all at once. Otherwise, you'll be like Dr. Jones—you will look wealthy on the outside, but you will obligate yourself to be working until you can't work anymore. Unfortunately, this is not as uncommon as you'd like to think. In fact, 28% of physicians age 60-65 do not have $1,000,000 in net worth (all assets - all debts).[17] That means a larger number (probably ~30-50%) can't retire at the age of 60. That's insanity.

The take home? Residents, fellows, and freshly minted attendings: take a small bump in lifestyle when you finish. I suggest 10% of your raise. Then, put the rest towards building wealth for two to three years. Your future self will thank you.

---

[17] Medscape. Physician Wealth and Debt Report 2018. https://www.medscape.com/slideshow/2018-physician-wealth-debt-report-6009863 Accessed January 25th, 2019.

Chapter 11:
Investing After Residency

"This gets to the heart of the investing process: The goal is not to maximize the chances of getting rich, but rather to simultaneously allow for a comfortable retirement and to minimize the odds of dying poor."
~ Dr. William J. Bernstein

At my little girl's golf practice one day, I got to talking to her coach. I asked him how he decided he wanted to be a golf coach.

"Well, I didn't always plan on this," he said. "Actually, I was going to be a financial advisor."

Of course, this piqued my interest and the natural follow-up question was to find out why he didn't finish pursuing this line of work. He proceeded to tell me the following story, which will be useful for you to remember in your journey interacting with the financial industry.

To land the financial advising job at the particular insurance company where he applied, he had to undergo several preliminary interviews. He made it through and landed a spot with two other people at the final interview day. When they arrived, they were instructed to write down ten names of family and friends. Their task was to "cold call" these ten people and sell them a financial product. When the future coach asked more about the product, the company representative said, "That's the point, you are going to be a salesperson … if you want to make a commission from a sale, then you need to be able to sell something whether you know a lot or a little about the product." When the future coach stood his ground and said that he could not endorse a product that he knew very little about, he was asked to leave. He was not invited back and—needless to say—he didn't get the job. This was his first real taste of the financial industry.

The reason that this chapter starts out with this story is to remind you that as a physician (or a physician in training), you have a giant target on your back. You are a gazelle running carefree in a field full of lions. Everyone views you as their next meal. Never forget that. If someone tries to sell you something that you don't understand, such as the latest and greatest individual security (i.e. stock), algorithm-based investing, hedge funds, or commodity-based securities, run the other way. When an insurance salesperson or advisor wants to meet with you to grant you access to special funds and stocks to which other people don't have access, simply say, "no thanks." At the very least, eat the free steak dinner and ignore everything they say. You'll be better off for it, and you'll be sure to avoid getting that phone call from a salesperson trying to make a commission off of your ignorance.

The Pareto Principle Remembered

While the prior chapters on student loan debt management might be the meat of this book, this chapter serves as the potatoes. In no other chapter am I going to preach the Pareto Principle more. The topic of investing has produced hundreds or thousands of books. There are many ways to skin a cat, but our goal is to create something that is easy to manage and easy to ignore. Clearly, we cannot cover the depth and breadth of this topic in a single chapter. Follow along, if you dare, as we discuss the 20% that you need to know to get 80% (or more) of the necessary results to reach financial independence.

Invest or Pay Down Debt

Before we can get to the bulk of the investing advice, we need to answer the most common question that I get from people, "Should I pay down my debt or invest in the market?" There are two sides to each argument, and I land pretty safely on the paying down debt side, but with a firm balance on investing. The reason that I land on this side is because being debt free provides several benofits. Here are a few:

1. The freedom of being out from underneath the burden of debt cannot be overstated. That is one less mandatory expense that would be necessary should you fall on rough times.
2. You save yourself the interest you would owe on the debt by paying it off early. Once the debt is gone, you can then use the payment you were making towards debt and put it towards investments.
3. Paying down debt is a guaranteed return on your money; if you invest, there is no guarantee that the market will do better than your interest rate on your loans. Also, once your debt is paid off, you can simply apply that previous payment towards investing.

To figure your debt-to-income ratio, simply divide your anticipated student loans at graduation by your anticipated annual income. Here are my guidelines for choosing whether you should pay down debt or invest, and in what order. If you find yourself in the middle (a debt-to-income ratio of 1-1.5, then you may have to figure out which route to take).

If your debt-to-income ratio is <1 (i.e. $250,000 in debt with $300,000 in annual income) -or- you are enrolled in PSLF, you have room to invest your money while you pay off debt

1. Max out your 401K/403B for both you and your spouse (if married) to at least receive all matches and contributions from your employer.
2. Make the above in a pre-tax fashion so you can put extra post-tax money towards your debt.
3. Max out your Health Savings Account (HSA) if you have a high deductible health care plan.
4. Max out any governmental 457 for you and your spouse, if you have one.
5. If not in PSLF, privately refinance and use any extra money towards destroying your debt.
6. Max out your Backdoor Roth IRA space for both you and your spouse (if married).
7. If in PSLF, make minimum payments and max out other investment vehicles (taxable account, etc.).

If your debt-to-income ratio is >1.5-2 (i.e. $450,000-$600,000 in debt; $300,000 in annual income), you should pay off your debt at all costs

1. Make sure you take advantage of PSLF, if you can! Starting PSLF now (even if you've missed out on previous payments) may still be the best choice.
2. Max out your pre-tax contributions to your 401K/403B for both you and your spouse (if married) to receive at least all matches and contributions from your employer. Otherwise, you leave part of your salary on the table.
3. If you are not doing PSLF, every extra dollar should go towards debt.

Four Keys to Investing Success

Now that we've handled the introductory question of paying off debt or investing, let's move onto investing basics. The essentials for investing can be summed up in four key goals: risk, diversification, time in the market, and minimizing fees.

Risk

This one is pretty simple. The more risk you take, the higher your potential reward. This is why buying a part of a company (i.e., stocks) usually provides a higher return than lending money that is owed to you at a later date (i.e., bonds). For example, if you speculated on Amazon back when they were just a company selling books and kept that stock until today, it would be worth a pretty penny. That's because investing in Amazon carried the risk of going completely bankrupt and you had the chance of losing every invested penny. If you think the chances of a company going belly-up are unlikely, then go back 50 years and look at the names of the 100 largest companies and see how many still exist today. The risk of failure for any individual company is high. Thus, they must pay you a high reward in return for your risk.

Given that I believe in a "set it and forget it" investing philosophy, our goal is to always optimize risk and reward. As the quote says at the beginning of this chapter, our goal isn't to get the best returns—our goal is to not die poor. We want to garner the reward of investing in stocks, but without the unmitigated risk. We don't need to feel the high of picking the individual winning stock and telling our friends that we got it right. What we want is the surest way to achieve our goals while minimizing risk. This means you have to invest in stocks, but not in individual stocks which carry unmitigated risks.

However, it is just as important to mention that if we are going to expect high rewards some years, then it is a foregone conclusion that we will experience bad losses in others. You must know deep down that a bear market is coming and that you could lose a third of your portfolio. In fact, a correction (i.e. 10% drop from most recent high in market) occurs once every 1.5 years. Imagining what that looks like in your head and actually seeing your $1,000,000 turn into $900,000 over a short period of time are two different experiences. What if a recession hits and that number becomes $650,000? You must understand that risk is part of the game and that, over a long investing timeline, the risk will pay off.

The market will come back up. And, if it doesn't, what you needed to invest in was guns, water, ammunition, and canned food.

Diversification

One way to gain the rewards of risk and investing in stocks while minimizing the disadvantages of risk is through diversification. The idea here is that by investing in multiple areas of the market, you can allow some of your stocks to soar while some of the others are tanking. One part zigs, the other part zags. A diversified portfolio provides balance and protection from market turmoil.

This is the reason that it isn't a good idea for most people to invest in individual stocks. Investing in individual stocks does not diversify away your risk. No matter how much research you put into a company or its stock, there are too many factors outside of the intrinsic value of a company that determine the stock price. Things like presidential elections, war, purported crimes by the CEO, and even natural disasters can change a stock price. It's simply a risk that's not worth taking.

A great example of this is the market collapse that occurred in Japan at the end of the 1980s. For years, people who invested in the market could earn 5-10 times what they had poured into their market. Anyone who was someone was investing in the Japanese economy. However, those whose entire portfolio had been invested in that market were sorely disappointed when the mountainside that had been the Japanese market crashed into a valley. An image of what this looked like is included below. Instead of continually

135

climbing returns, people were lucky to break even 15 or 20 years later.

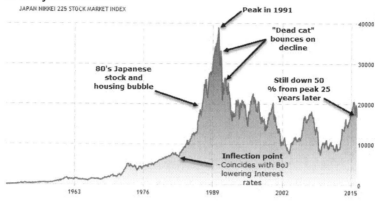

Source: http://thenudeinvestor.com/stock-market-crashes-are-we-about-to-experience-one-what-history-can-tell-us/

Investors who exclusively invested in the Japanese market (and were not diversified into other economies) paid a steep price. This is just one example of many. The same can be said of those who had disproportionate shares of other bubbles that burst, including the tulip bulb craze, the tech bubble, the dot-com bubble, or the housing bubble. The key to avoid all of this, of course, is to diversify your risk so that when one portion of your investments is doing poorly, the others are hopefully doing well.

Time in the market

Time in the market is more important than timing the market. In fact, timing the market – or trying to buy when the market is "low" and sell when the market is "high" – should never be your goal. We should be spending our time taking good care of patients and not trying to determine when the market is going to bottom out. If we invest in a diversified portfolio that provides enough risk to gain reward, then we should be able to leave our money in and just let it grow. Time in the market is going to be your friend and it is a financial must to avoid one of the catastrophes that will sink our financial ship: Buying high and selling low.

Several people have performed studies to show the importance of staying in the market to your investing success. Burton Malkiel, the author of *A Random Walk on Wall Street*, says it this way:

Buy and hold investors in the U.S. stock market made an average annual return of 8% during the 15 years from 1995 through 2009. But if they had missed the 30 best days in the market over that period, their return would have been negative.[18]

Did you catch that? Just 30 days missed over a 15-year period would produce a negative return, while staying in the market would have produced an 8% growth on your money. Other companies and studies have shown the same finding multiple times over various time periods in the market. This is why time in the market is one of the biggest keys to your investing success. Market corrections, recessions, and even depressions are going to happen. Don't worry about them. Expect them, and then stay in the market.

Just stick to the plan. If you can't, then remember to have your best friend sign in to all of your accounts, set your password, and have them promise to never tell it

---

[18] Malkiel, B. Burton Malkiel author of "A Random Walk on Wall Street" Defends Buy and Hold.
http://awmfinancial.com/uncategorized/burton-malkiel-author-of-a-random-walk-down-wall-street-defends-buy-and-hold/ Accessed January 25th, 2019.

to you. That would ultimately be better for you than taking the risk of selling something when you get nervous. It'll be a strange feeling going from wanting to punch your friend in the face during a down market, to thanking them profusely when it comes back up. Pay them in whatever way you feel is appropriate. They've likely earned it.

Minimizing fees

One of the biggest determinants of long-term success while investing is the cost of investing, which is usually determined by fees. Any time you purchase a fund or an individual security such as a stock, there is an associated fee. There are too many fees to count, but let's name the important ones: transaction fees, expense ratios, and financial advising fees.

Expense ratios are what each fund charges to manage the fund. For actively managed funds, this includes the hedge fund manager's salary, 12B-1 fees for advertising, and turnover costs for buying/selling stocks. The industry standard for an actively managed mutual fund is an expense ratio of 1%. Over one year, this may not cost you much, but over decades it will cost you millions with the amount of money you should be investing as a doctor. Let's look at some math. Say you invest $50,000 each year. Your portfolio earns 8% in the market over 30 years. You'll have $4.38 million dollars. Now subtract out your 1% expense ratio, and you've earned 7% over that same time frame. You've now earned $3.79 million dollars. How much has that cost you? $590,000. With rough math, that's an extra ten years of work to save the extra $500,000 ($50,000 per year for ten years).

The reason the above is a conservative estimate is because many people should be saving more. I recommend 20-30% of your gross income. So, if you are making $300,000 per year, you should be saving $60,000-90,000. If you want financial independence in your 40s, it may be even more. Say, for example you invested $75,000 per year, instead of the $50,000 given in the first example, that 1% expense ratio will cost you $880,000 over 30 years. That's a lot of money, and we aren't even counting retirement time, when that number will exceed $1.5 million. If you can get the same return or better out of a fund with a lower expense ratio, you'll save a lot of money (You can do this. It is called an index fund, where the industry standard expense ratio is <0.1%, or 1/10th of the industry standard expense ratio for actively managed funds.)

Here is the most important cost to keep down, the cost of financial advising. If you are using an Assets Under Management (AUM) financial advisor that charges 1% and placing you into actively managed mutual funds with expense ratios of 1%, then you can double the amount of money that would cost. If you are bad at math, that 2% (1% to the actively managed fund; 1% to your advisor) will cost around $1.2 million dollars over 30 years in the $50,000 example above. For the $75,000 example, it will cost you around $1.8 million dollars. You better love your job, because that's a lot of extra years worked to make up all of that money you have lost on fees and financial advising.

Let me take the time to say that I am *not* anti-financial advisor. Some people need or want financial help from a professional. If you fit that bill, what you are looking for is a flat fee-only advisor (not a fee-based advisor) operating as a fiduciary who has experience with physicians.

This is why it pays to know the 20% you need to know. Your best bet to keep fees down and to get the average market return is to passively invest in low-cost index funds in the asset classes of your choosing. If you absolutely must get financial advice you should pay for it as flat rate advice from a fee-only advisors who has experience with physicians. This may feel like it costs you more up front, but it is a fair price and once the work is done, the flat-fee advisor will release you to do things yourself. So, unlike the AUM model which gets paid out of your assets each year, flat fee-only advisors only cost you whenever you actually need them. If you need recommended financial advisors that fill the bill, you can find them on The Physician Philosopher website.

Automatic Wealth Building

As I've said before, the biggest determinant of your success depends on your ability to get out of your own way. In our country, it is common to spend the money that you are paid. We are consumers at heart. So, the best way to protect ourselves from spending all of the money we have is to make our wealth-building automatic.

What I mean is this: pay your future self first and your current self last. Before you even see your paycheck, the money you are going to use to build wealth should come out first. Just like tithing, if you believe in that. Here is an example of what that looked like in my first year as an attending physician. The numbers are approximations and include both my wife's part time-teacher income and my income, but are accurate enough to prove the point.

Take home: $15,000
($1,541.66 pre-tax to 403B)
($1,500 pre-tax governmental 457)
-$1,600 post-tax tithe to church
-$5,500 student loan payment
<u>-$1,100 college fund (529) for three kids</u>
$6,800 dollars

So, while my wife and I make a lot more than we did in residency, almost all of this money is directed to a certain place before we even see it. From that $6,800 we have to then take out our mortgage ($750), car payments ($1,000), life insurance ($150), auto insurance ($300), childcare ($750), utilities (~$250), and food for a family of five (~$1,500). After all of those relatively fixed expenses, we only have $2,100 left for the more discretionary spending—vacations, golf, movies, kids' activities (like karate/ballet/sports), etc. You can imagine that if all of these payments came out first, I might not be as disciplined about putting money towards building wealth.

This is the reason that you must pay your future self first and your current self last. My take home pay could be higher if we didn't invest in my 403B or my wife's governmental 457, but we would probably just waste it on golf, vacations, and manicures if we saw more of the money in our bank account. Understanding behavioral finance is probably 90% of the game. You need to never see the money and just accept that it is going towards future goals. If you need motivation, imagine the debt-free life you'll be living at an early age. Consider that money untouchable. If the budget is too tight, then change your lifestyle. Don't decrease the money going towards building wealth.

My Investing Philosophy

When you invest, there are many ways to skin the cat. That said, I am a "set it and forget it" kind of guy for two reasons.

1. Research has shown that the more you check your portfolio, the more likely you are to make changes, and the worse you will likely do in the market. As long as you are not speculating on individual stocks (which is the opposite of set it and forget it), time in the market is what leads to success.

2. Your job is to learn and practice medicine so that you can take care of other people. You should not be spending a boatload of time trying to figure all of this stuff out. Just learn the 20% you have to know. Then, focus on taking care of patients. Could you make more by slanting your asset allocation towards value and small cap stocks? Probably, but that would require more work that is likely not worth the time. The investing philosophy we are about to discuss allows you to do well and to put your focus where it should be.

For any of you who would rather invest in actively managed funds that are run by professionals, let's look at the track record to put this thing to bed. Actively managed funds *can* outperform index funds. But what are the odds you pick the right fund and that fund continues to outperform index funds over the next 5-10 years? The odds are exceedingly low. The 2017 SPIVA scorecard, which tracks such questions, has shown that over the last 15 years index funds have outperformed their actively managed mutual fund counterparts 92.33% of the time for large cap funds, 94.81% of the time for mid-cap funds, and almost 96% of the time for small cap funds.[19] That's a damning record no matter how you look at it. For those that don't know, "cap" means "capitalization." So, large cap index funds refer to the largest companies in the market. Small cap funds refer to the smallest companies. This is determined by each company's amount of capital. Mid cap funds usually have a capitalization between $2 million and $10 million. Small caps have < $2million and large caps have >$10 million.

Speculation (i.e. investing in bitcoin, tulip bulbs, or any other individual stock) is the exact opposite of "set it and forget it." The required research to perform technical analysis (i.e. looking at market trends) or fundamental analysis (i.e. looking at various independent factors for each investment) –both of which have major flaws –prevents you from letting the most important aspect of investing work: time in the market.

Index funds are the easiest way to diversify risk, simplify investing, and avoid your worst enemies: the financial industry and yourself. As John Templeton, a British stock investor, said, "The four most expensive

---

[19] SPIVA scorecard.
https://us.spindices.com/documents/spiva/spiva-us-year-end-2017.pdf Accessed October 19th, 2018.

words in the English language are '*This time it's different.*'" Just get out of your own way and invest in broadly diversified index funds.

Investment Vehicles

Any discussion on the 20% of investing you need to know should include investment vehicles. It is no good if I tell you what to invest in, but do not tell you where and how to invest the money. To do this, a discussion on taxes is required.

Your money can be taxed at three different phases in the game. First, your money can be taxed before it is invested. Common examples of "post-tax" investments include taxable accounts and Roth accounts. The interest earned in the account can also be taxed on the growth when you sell it. An example of this is short and long-term capital gains taxes in a taxable account. Finally, it can also be taxed when you take it out. Examples of this include pre-tax retirement accounts such as Traditional IRAs, 401Ks, 403Bs, and 457s.

Taxes play a large part in the investing game, but one could write an entire book on taxes. Given that tax law changes annually, it will not be covered here. Suffice it to say you want less tax-efficient investments (i.e. actively managed funds, most bonds, REITs, preferred stocks, etc.) in your retirement accounts and more tax-efficient investments (index funds, municipal bonds, etc.) in your taxable account. Information beyond this is likely in the 80% that you don't need to know right now.

Speaking of the Pareto Principle, here are the steps for sorting this out:

1. Calculate your number for financial independence (discussed in chapter 12).
2. Determine your timeline so that you are able to retire when you want.
3. Figure out how much you need to save annually to get there. An online calculator is often helpful for this.
4. Finally, use that number and max out your investment accounts in the following order as you have money to invest:
   a. 401K/403B
   b. Health savings account (HSA)
   c. Governmental 457
   d. Backdoor Roth IRA
   e. Consider non-governmental 457 (if it meets criteria below and works for your needs)
   f. Taxable account

**Cash balance plans discussed separately

Retirement vehicle number 1: 401K/403B

Your 401K (or 403B, we will discuss them interchangeably) is the first place that money should go. One reason is that it is tax advantaged space (it decreases your taxable income). If you are employed, you may also receive an investment "match" from your employer in your 401K. For example, if your employer matches 4% of your income and your income is

$200,000, then your employer will match the first $8,000 you put into your 401K (or 4% of your income). If you don't take this opportunity, you are leaving money on the table.

These two retirement vehicles are most likely offered by your employer. By and large, the 401K and 403B can be viewed identically. The reason for their name is from the specific section of the Internal Revenue Service tax code from which they originate (i.e., section 401K). As of 2019, the employee contribution limit for 401K/403Bs is $19,000 (until age 50 when you can contribute $25,000). Your employer can then contribute or match up to a max of $56,000 ($62,000 with catch-up after age 50).

The 20% you need to know about the 401K and 403B is to use them identically. When you set up a 401K/403B, it is common to have to choose to invest the money "pre-tax" (standard) or "post-tax" (Roth). While there is some debate on this issue, most would tell you that it is wise to put your money into a 401K/403B using a pre-tax method during your peak earning years (i.e., as an attending physician) and via a Roth method in your non-peak earning years (i.e., residency, fellowship, and part-time work at the end of your career). Roth vehicles do come with some major advantages, but that is outside the scope of this book.

Before we end our discussion on the 401K, it needs to be said that this option is available for self-contracted physicians (i.e., those being paid on a 1099). For these doctors, you simply need to look into opening an individual 401K, sometimes called a "solo 401K." Most of the big financial companies offer this vehicle, which is a better option than a SEP-IRA because the solo 401K allows you to take part in a Backdoor Roth IRA without getting crushed by the *pro rata rule*.

Retirement vehicle number 2: Health Savings Account (HSA)

The Health Savings Account (HSA) is a great option for people with high-deductible health insurance plans. Given that I want this book to be helpful even in the setting of changing laws, I won't include any numbers in this book. Just search the internet for HSA requirements to see if your health insurance plan qualifies. Alternatively, you could just ask your employer's human resources (HR) department. As of 2019, you can place $7,000 of your pre-tax money into this account if you are married ($3,500 if single).

The HSA is a great option because it offers the best tax advantage of any retirement account. It is triple tax-free. Money is placed into the account pre-tax, it grows tax free, and it is not taxed when taken out as long as it is used on health care expenditures. In baseball, that would be called a grand slam, and it is the reason that you should max this thing out every year. That said, it's your employer's job to make the HSA enticing enough over the other options.

For those who are worried that they won't have enough medical bills to justify using an HSA, let's discuss three reasons that this line of thinking falls short. First, if receipts are saved from medical expenses, they can be turned in at a later date to let your HSA grow. You do not have to collect on the money spent immediately. Second, health care costs in our golden years account for a high percentage of the costs we incur. Third, if your family doesn't ever have enough medical care to justify an HSA, you can thank your lucky stars and take the money out penalty-free after the age of 65. The only tax you have to pay is income tax on your distribution. If you used it in this way, it would function as yet another pre-tax 401K/403B.

Retirement vehicle number 3: The 457 (deferred compensation) plan

While a 401K is pretty straightforward, the same cannot be said for the 457 plan. Blanket statements do not apply for this plan, because not everyone should be investing in it. Like a 401K, you can contribute $19,000 into this account.   There is no employer match, however.

The 457 plan comes in different shapes and varieties. The two major 457 plans are governmental 457s and non-governmental 457s (NG 457s). Below are the differences between the two. If you don't care to know, the breakdown is simple: you should almost always use governmental 457 investment vehicles. Whether or not to use a non-governmental 457 is much more complicated. If you have the latter, then keep reading to figure it all out.

Governmental 457s versus NG-457s
(Reference IRS publication)[20]

- Governmental 457s may be rolled over to eligible retirement plans such as an IRA (NG-457 plans do not permit rollovers).
- Age > 50 catch-up contributions are only available for governmental 457s.
- NG-457 "top-hat" plans must limit the number of people who can participate to "groups of highly compensated employees or groups of executives, managers, directors or officers."
- Governmental 457s often allow Roth contributions. NG-457s do not allow Roth contributions.
- *This is the most important difference*: Governmental 457s are backed by the US government (NG-457s are backed by individual institutions and are available to creditors upon legal action or bankruptcy). This is the exact wording from the IRS on NG-457s[21]:

    "[Non-governmental] plan assets are not held in trust for employees, but remain the property of the employer (available to its general creditors in the event of litigation or bankruptcy) ... Employees are lower in priority than general creditors in the event of legal claims against the employer."

---

[20] This is the referenced IRS publication in the hyperlink above: https://www.irs.gov/pub/irs-pdf/p4484.pdf
[21] IRS website. https://www.irs.gov/retirement-plans/non-governmental-457b-deferred-compensation-plans . Accessed January 26, 2019.

What this last bullet point means is that if your institution goes bankrupt or into major litigation, your hard-earned retirement money is available to creditors. This is very different from your typical 401K or 403B which is protected even in the case of most personal litigation (i.e., medical malpractice) or employment catastrophe (i.e., your institution goes bankrupt).

When should you participate in a 457?

I'll answer the chip shot first. Every employee with access to a governmental 457 should take part. For those who plan to retire early, a governmental 457 would even be preferred to a 401K/403B. Why? Unlike a 401K/403B, a 457 plan can be accessed before age 59.5 without getting hit with a 10% penalty. You just have to leave your employer. Either way, a governmental 457 can be viewed as a second 401K or 403B.

If you have a NG-457, you need to be intimately familiar with the plan before you take part. Also, you should contribute to your 401K/403B, Health Savings Account (HSA), and Roth IRA before you take part in your non-governmental 457. When you have filled up all of your other tax-advantaged retirement space, should you invest in the 457 offered by your employer over a typical taxable account?

In my opinion, a NG-457 must offer all of the following before I would recommend taking part in the plan rather than simply investing in a taxable account. If the plan doesn't have all three of these features, you should consider investing in a taxable account.

- Investors must be very familiar with the financial security of their institution. Because this money is available to creditors should the institution go bankrupt, investors should determine how likely they think that bankruptcy is based on what they know. Otherwise, they might be in for some sleepless nights.
- The NG-457 plan must have good distribution options. Many NG-457 plans have terrible options, such as a lump sum option that requires the investor to inherit a giant tax bill when they leave the employer or retire. Don't invest in a NG-457 with bad distribution options. Remember, unlike a governmental 457, you cannot roll your NG-457 into an IRA. You need to check into all of the options for distribution. What you are looking for is a long time frame to receive the money (10-20 years) so that you can avoid the big tax bill.
- It must have good investment options, such as low-cost index funds. If the only thing they are offering is actively managed hedge funds with expense ratios of 2%, then you probably shouldn't play that game. Prefer a taxable account in that situation.

Retirement vehicle number 4:
Roth individual retirement account (IRA)

If you are reading this book and still in training, this is the first account to fill up because you can still directly contribute to the Roth IRA without worrying about income limits. What happens when our income goes above the Roth IRA limit?

Let me introduce the "backdoor Roth IRA." For those who haven't heard of this method of investing, here are some of the basics. The government allows you to put $6,000 (2019 rules) into a traditional IRA each year for both you and your spouse even if you or your spouse do not have earned income. Say, for example, if my wife was an orthopedic surgeon and I was a stay-at-home dad with no earned income. We could still invest $6,000 for both of us, or $12,000 total.

However, there is another kind of IRA in which you can invest, which is called a Roth IRA. Anytime you see the word "Roth" you should think "post-tax." It's just a specific kind of vehicle. The advantage to placing post-tax money into a retirement account is that it has already been taxed, which means it will grow tax free and will not be taxed when it is taken out years later. That includes any money inherited by your heirs. They won't be taxed on it either. As we previously mentioned in the example we gave for why it's worth it to invest as a resident, you should always touch Roth money last in retirement.

As of the writing of this book, if you make more than $137,000 (single) or $203,000 (married), you cannot directly contribute to a Roth IRA. However, you can contribute to a traditional IRA (no income limits) and then perform a Roth conversion, because the government has no income limits on conversions. I know. It's confusing. The government limits contributions, but not conversions. The gist is that you can contribute $6,000 to a traditional IRA and then immediately convert it to a Roth IRA. If you want a specific tutorial on how to perform your first backdoor Roth, I've written a step-by-step tutorial on my website.

One other item that I should discuss is the *pro rata rule*. So that I won't get into the 80% of stuff you don't need to know, suffice it to say that you have to pay a big tax bill that wipes out any advantage of a backdoor Roth IRA if you have any other IRA money. This includes a Simplified Employee Pension IRA (SEP-IRA), simple IRA, or rollover IRA. This is the reason that physician finance-savvy folks don't recommend a SEP-IRA for income earned on the side. Those with self-employed incomes should use a solo-401K instead, which doesn't count against you in the pro rata rule. For the same reason, don't use a rollover IRA when you change employers, because this will count against you in the pro rata calculation. What should you do with your 401K if you change employers? Your choices are to leave it your current 401K, transfer it to your next employer's 401K, or earn some side income and open a solo-401K that you can roll it into.

Retirement vehicle number 5:
Taxable accounts

The taxable account has a terrible name. It makes it sound like an awful investment vehicle. All that "taxable" means is that you are placing money into the account that has already been taxed. The contribution doesn't get taxed again, but any earnings will get taxed at either the short-term capital gains tax (i.e., taxed at your marginal tax rate if held for less than one year) or the long-term capital gains tax (if sold after holding longer than one year). If you are in a high-income tax bracket, then long-term capital gains taxes are usually lower than short-term capital gains taxes.

One important advantage of a taxable account is that it is the most readily accessible investment vehicle. There are a lot more rules involved in accessing money from a 401K, 403B, 457, and IRA. With a taxable account, you simply sell the shares to get the money you need. Again, the contributions aren't taxed, but the gains will be taxed according to how long you've held that share.

Outside of the flexibility, are there other reasons to invest in a taxable account? The short answer is that you might have more money left that you want to invest, and this is the only choice that is left. Say for example, you determine that you want to save $4 million for retirement. You are 35 and want to retire at 55. In order to get to $4 million (assuming you are earning 7% on average over the 20 years), you'd have to save just under $100,000 per year. Let's fill that money up to show you why you need a taxable account.

Yearly savings goal = $100,000
$56,000 401K max
$19,000 governmental 457
$12,000 backdoor Roth IRA
<u>$7,000 HSA</u>
$6,000 left to invest

So, even if you fill up a ton of tax advantaged space, you'll still need a taxable account to get to your $100,000 annual investment goal. If you do not have all of this tax advantaged space available to you for one reason or another, then you will need to place even more money into a taxable account.

Early in your career you may not have enough money to invest because of the need to pay down debt. I didn't start investing in a taxable account until all of my student loan debt was gone. Prior to that, I did not have the capital to invest into a taxable account. That's what happens when you pay off $200,000 in less than twenty months.

Where can you get a taxable account? Any of the major investment companies (Vanguard, Charles Schwab, Fidelity, etc.) will be able to set you up with one. Figure out which one you like best that offers low-cost index fund investing (all three of the ones I mentioned provide this), because index funds are very tax efficient, which is important in a taxable account. Then, like any other investments, automatically draft your money from your paycheck each month to the taxable account.

One area where you don't want to "Set it and forget it" with taxable accounts is with tax loss harvesting. I won't get into the nitty gritty here, but it's worth mentioning briefly. The idea is that when you have a bad investing period, you can sell your funds at a loss. You then report that loss on your taxes and get to "harvest it." (You should not do this in a retirement account because you pay a 10% penalty if you take money out early from a retirement account.) Then, you buy something that is not "substantially identical" but is another index fund tracking a similarly size index. You use this loss to either reduce future capital gains taxes or to reduce your ordinary income. There is a wealth of information on tax loss harvesting out on the internet; I just want to introduce you to the idea if you have not previously heard of it.

Retirement vehicle number 6:
Cash Balance Plans

Cash balance plans are another form of tax-advantaged retirement space, similar to a 401K. However, whereas a 401K plan is a defined contribution (i.e., there are defined limits you can contribute), a cash balance plan is a defined benefit plan (like a pension). The reason that this discussion on cash balance plans has been left for last is that it is much more complicated, and it is not available to everyone. In fact, cash balance plans are usually only available to private practice physicians who own their own group.

These plans can be complicated, but my job here is to simplify things. So, here is the 20% you need to know about cash balance plans in case your future employer offers one:

- Cash balance plans can be rolled into a 401K or IRA upon leaving the employer.
- The amount that can be placed into a cash balance plan is dictated by actuarial tables and the age of participants. Generally, the older the participants, the more money that can be tucked away inside the cash balance plan. This can vary widely. It is not always a great thing to participate in a cash balance plan when young.
- The money placed into the account is technically from the employer, not from the employee.
- You have less control over the investments that are chosen within this plan—it is typically

designed and run by a company outside of the private practice.

- The plan can require you to put additional money into the account if the returns are not stellar. This additional money is tax deductible.
- Given the complexity required to run a cash balance plan, expenses are often much higher than in a typical 401K plan.
- If a cash balance plan exists at your workplace, you will be required to participate, though the required amount is often much lower than the maximum amount that can be placed into the plan. For example, you might be required to put in $5,000 per year with the opportunity to contribute as much as $20,000.

All told, the cash balance plan is another way to sock away money in a pre-tax fashion in order to save for retirement. While it decreases your tax burden and can dramatically increase the amount participants are able to put away each year, it is also much more complicated than a 401K plan. Do your homework before taking part.

The 529 Account

If you are interested in putting money away for college education for your children, here is a primer on 529 accounts. Money placed into these accounts is post-tax money that is treated similarly to a Roth IRA account. The money has already been taxed, which means it will not be taxed again. Like a Roth IRA account (and unlike a taxable account), the growth that occurs is also not taxed again as long as it is used on educational expenses. For this reason, the 529 plan is a great vehicle to save for college education expenses, and a great way to earmark an account specifically for this purpose.

Should you invest in a 529? That is a deeply personal question. First, determine whether you will pay your children's college expenses. If you do decide to pay for your child's college education, this should not happen at the cost of saving for retirement. You should not have to choose between the two. A 529 should be funded only once you have a clear path to financial independence. If your child had to choose between having college paid or paying for your lodging and care in your elderly years because you didn't save enough; well, the choice would be easy. Give them the student loans. But if you look at the numbers and see that you will clearly reach FI by the age you want, then by all means put money into a 529 (if you believe paying for your child's college education is the right thing to do).

You do not have to invest in your own state's 529 plan, but it is helpful to look to see if your state offers tax benefits for investing in their 529. If no tax breaks exist, then you are free to take part in 529 plans offered by other states. In my opinion, some of the states that offer the best plans with low-cost index funds and low management fees include Utah, Nevada, and Virginia (my wife and I use the Utah My 529 plan for our three kids). As things often change, do your due diligence and make sure that this remains the same at the time that you read this book.

Also, it is worth mentioning four specific features of 529 plans:

1. If the person for whom the 529 is intended earns scholarship money, an equal amount can be taken out of the 529 tax-and penalty-free). For example, if your daughter won a $10,000 scholarship, then $10,000 could be removed from the 529 without penalty to be used for other expenses. The growth in the account will be taxed, however.
2. Speaking of penalties, any money taken out that is not used on educational expenses does incur one. The penalty as of this writing is similar to that which occurs on early 401K/403B withdrawals: income tax on any earnings in the account plus a 10% penalty.
3. The name of the person who is anticipated to use the 529 plan can be changed to another person. Say, for example, your kid decided not to go to college or signed up for the military. This is not a problem. The 529 plan can be renamed to another child, grandchild, niece, nephew, or friend's kid.
4. Yes, a 529 plan counts against your child when they apply for federal aid, but so does your high-income. So, unless you plan to not be working by the time they go to college, it is a fool's errand to make the argument not to fund a 529 for this reason.

Stock-to-bond Ratio

When you take a Caribbean cruise, you expect the captain of the ship to do more than just get you to your destination. You also expect the captain to get you there safely and comfortably. Traveling while nervous that your boat might capsize, hit an iceberg, or make you seasick isn't fun for anyone. For this reason, most cruise ships have advanced stabilizer technology that limits the amount a boat can list from side to side. The entire purpose is to make your ride smoother. This is exactly how you can think about bonds. They are there to get you to your goal, to keep you afloat, and to prevent you from drowning by inflation.

A bond is money lended to a company, government, or municipality that they promise to pay back. You become the lender and the bond issuer becomes the borrower, paying you back on interest called a "yield." There are many different kinds of bonds ranging from junk bonds (high risk; high possible return) to U.S. Treasury bonds (low risk; low return). Lower risk bonds—treasury bonds, Treasury Inflation Protected Securities (TIPS), and municipal bonds, for example— provide a relatively guaranteed return on your money. This is the portion of your money that you can count on when the market tanks. The more bonds you have in your portfolio, the less risk and the lower return you receive; but you also enjoy more safety and security of your money. Just like a cruise ship.

A stock, on the other hand, is more like owning a portion of a speed boat that is lined up in a race. In the race, a speed boat will make it to your destination faster than would a cruise ship, but that reward comes with more risk. Along the way, the speed boat is more likely to wreck, capsize, or make you seasick.

Stocks provide you a share in a company. In other words, if you decide to buy a company's stock, then you become part owner of that company. You take on all the risks and benefits of ownership. If the company explodes with growth, you make a lot of money. If it goes bankrupt, you lose everything you invested. You can see why having an asset allocation with only stocks is problematic. It involves too much risk.

The balance of stocks (speed boats) and bonds (cruise ships) in your portfolio needs to accomplish the following:
1. It must provide a certain amount of security to you so that you will not sell in a bear (down) market.
2. The security provided by the percentage of bonds must also allow you to "set and forget" your portfolio so that you check it as infrequently as possible.
3. The percentage of stocks in your portfolio must provide enough diversified risk that you can plan on getting an acceptable return from the market. Too little risk means too little return to accomplish your goals.
4. You need to be able to sleep at night, knowing that your plan is made and you just need to stick to it.

Exactly what that split should be for each person is tough to say. It is commonly recommended to have a much larger proportion of stocks to bonds when you have a long investing timeline, such as when you are in your 20s. As you age, you will want to take less risk by increasing the proportion of bonds in your portfolio. Remember, the idea behind buying bonds is that they provide more security, but also a lower reward. As you age, you want to take less risk because, hopefully, you've made your number by that point. What you are trying to do then is to simply keep up with inflation. The rule of thumb here is to have the same percentage of bonds as your age (i.e. a 30-year-old should have 30% bonds and 70% stocks).

Regardless of how you choose to invest, understand that risks are often rewarded over a long investing timeline. However, risk can be quite dangerous if you need the money now. When the 2008/2009 depression hit, investors who were 100% stocks likely lost around half of their portfolios. Of course, that was perfectly fine if you had a long investing timeline and could tolerate waiting for the stock values to climb out of the pit to where they are today. But if your portfolio was 100% stocks and you had planned to retire that year, losing half of your portfolio would have provided some very real pain. Having some U.S. Treasury-backed bonds (which actually gained money) during that same time frame would have eased at least some of that pain.

Because I want this book to be practical, here is a guide. Consider adjusting these numbers based on your risk tolerance.
1. In your 30s, invest 80% stocks/20% bonds and remember to keep most of your bonds (except municipal bonds) in your retirement accounts as opposed to your taxable accounts.
2. At age 40, transition to 70% stocks/30% bonds.
3. At age 50, you'll need more bonds, depending on when you want to retire (potentially 40-50%)

Given the target audience of this book and the fact that explaining drawdown plans for retirement and retirement planning would require a book unto itself, I'll stop here. Everyone is so different in terms of their ability to tolerate risk that getting more specific might be difficult and even unhelpful at this early juncture. Just remember, you need to be able to sleep at night. Pick an asset allocation that allows you to rest easy.

A little more information

For those interested in knowing a little more about stocks and bonds, know that by and large, stocks are considered riskier investments and bonds are safer. However, the situation here is high risk, high reward. In other words, if you are going to take a greater risk, you should be compensated for this. Why are stocks higher risk (and higher reward)? The risk is two-fold. First, for each company that you are a part-owning stockholder, you carry the risk that the company could take off and become highly successful, or it could just as easily plummet into a stock value of zero dollars, where you lose all of your money. If you don't think this is likely, realize that only 12%, or a total of 60 out of 500, of the 500 largest companies in America in 1956 still remained in the top 500 fifty years later in 2016.[22] High risk; high reward. The second risk is that when companies begin to fail and must pay back people they owe money to, they are required by law to pay bondholders before stockholders. Thus, if they run out of money, stock holders (who get nothing back) are impacted more than are bondholders. This typically makes bonds less risky, but also explains why they provide a lower return.

---

[22] While I do not necessarily endorse other facts found on this site, this Is the source for that above information: http://www.aei.org/publication/fortune-500-firms-1955-v-2016-only-12-remain-thanks-to-the-creative-destruction-that-fuels-economic-prosperity/

This is why it is very important to have the right proportion of stocks and bonds in your portfolio. The safer the "company" you are getting a bond from is, the more likely you are to get your return. This explains why U.S. Governmental Treasury bonds are considered the safest kind of bond that exists. After all, it should be highly unlikely that the government collapses.

Asset Allocation

The percentage of stocks and bonds or small-cap stocks to large-cap stocks in your portfolio is called asset allocation. In other words, asset allocation is the percentage of your portfolio invested in various securities. Your goals are efficiency and diversification, because the more diversified your portfolio, the less susceptible you are to specific market downturns. It's really about mitigating risk. We want the highest reward for the least risk. This section of the book hopes to help you do that while still making it as simple as possible.

We will discuss asset allocation in terms of which funds to possess first. Then, we will discuss the mixture of stocks and bonds in your portfolio. The following simply serve as examples of how simple it can be despite how complicated others might make it sound.

The Boglehead's three fund portfolio

How simple can index fund investing be? Well, Taylor Larimore (one of the original followers of John "Jack" Bogle, the man who created Vanguard), has read pretty much every financial book out there and has come to recommend a three-fund portfolio that captures a piece of all of the market. It can be that easy.[23] What are the three funds?

- Stocks: Total Stock Market Index Fund (Examples: VTSMX, SWTSX, FSTMX, FSTVX)
- Stocks: Total International Stock Market Index Fund (Examples: VGTSX, SWISX, FTIGX, FTIPX)
- Bonds: Total Bond Market Fund (Examples: VBMFX, SWAGX, FBIDX, FSITX)

The Bernstein "no-brainer" fund

This is just an example. But it is helpful given that not all employers offer the funds listed above. Dr. William Bernstein, a neurologist turned financial advisor, offers a similar "no-brainer" portfolio that consists of investing in index funds in four key asset classes, all in index funds:

- 25% total bond index fund
- 25% European stocks index fund
- 25% small-cap value index fund
- 25% S&P (large-cap) index fund

What if those aren't options?

Of course, different employers offer different options. For example, my current employer doesn't give us access to the total stock market index fund, but they do offer other index funds. So, my job is to try and mirror

---

[23] Larimore T, Bogle J. *The Boglehead's Guide to the Three Fund Portfolio. How a Simple Portfolio of Three Total Market Index Funds Outperforms Most Investors with Less Risk.* Wiley; 1 edition (July 3, 2018)

the diversification shown above in my 403B and 457. I do this by picking an asset allocation that approximates something similar to the above mixture. I do not know the specific index fund company your employer uses, or if they have them all. If they do, they usually will have index funds broken up into individual asset classes if they don't offer the funds listed above. For example, it could look something like this:

- 25% large-cap index fund
- 10% mid-cap index fund
- 20% small-cap index fund
- 20% international stock market index fund
- 25% bond market index fund

Take a Peek Occasionally (Rebalancing Your Assets)

Once a year, take a peek at your investments to make sure that they are still mirroring your desired asset allocation. This is called rebalancing. The purpose of rebalancing is to keep your portfolio diversified, and because rebalancing usually—though not always—increases returns over the long haul. Just because one class has done well over the last year or two doesn't mean it will continue to do well. Stick to the plan and rebalance back to your pre-chosen asset allocation. There are two different techniques here (time-based and band-based rebalancing). Either one is fine. Just pick one.

Time-based rebalancing

The time-based rebalancing technique simply says that every year or two you look at your portfolio and then rebalance it to make it look like the asset allocation you decided on above. If anything is outside of 5% above or below your desired asset allocation, then you correct it by buying and selling.

For example, if you want 30% large caps and the large caps have exploded and are now 40% of your portfolio, you will sell some of your large caps and buy some of the other index funds in the other classes that didn't perform so well. This may make you concerned about the tax implications. In your retirement accounts (401K, 403B, 457, IRA) you can buy and sell (i.e. "trade") as much as you want because you are not actualizing any returns until you sell them for cash in retirement.

However, in a taxable account these concerns are founded. When you sell something there, you are likely going to get hit with a capital gains tax. That said, it's not a big deal. If you can rebalance things by buying and selling inside of your retirement accounts, that is preferred. If you must rebalance stuff in your taxable account, just do it efficiently. And, remember, you can tax-loss harvest any losses inside of a taxable account to save on future taxes. Take advantage of that, if possible.

It should be mentioned that as you are dumping money into accounts that are not very large early in your career, one very efficient way of rebalancing is simply changing your contributions into the account. For example, using the same example as above, say you have 40% in large-cap index funds after a good year, but your asset allocation calls for them to be around 30%. In that situation, you could simply change your next set of contributions to purchase more of the international index fund that hasn't done as well and choose to only place 25% of your contribution into large-cap index funds until you get back to your pre-chosen asset allocation. This is a good way to avoid the taxes that would be incurred by trading within a taxable account. You could also consider selling losers by tax-loss harvesting as previously discussed.

Band-based rebalancing

Band-based rebalancing says that anytime something goes above or below a certain percentage of your desired asset allocation (say, again, 5%), then you rebalance. I personally don't love this technique as much because it encourages you to look at your portfolio more often. As I've stated before, I am a fan of "set it and forget it" investing. This style of rebalancing implies that you are going to keep a closer eye on your portfolio, which isn't usually a good thing. But I do want you to know this exists, because it is an option that may be preferred by some of you.

Take Home

We covered a lot in this chapter! Here are the salient points:

- Determine how much you need to save each year to retire by the age you would like. Then fill up the buckets available to you to save that number.
- Your goals are to max out your tax advantaged retirement space when available, keep costs low, pay yourself last (automatic payments), diversify your risk, and take part in a "set it and forget it" method of investing.

- It doesn't have to be complicated and can be as simple as three or four funds.
- Pick an asset allocation that works for you and lets you sleep at night, while still being risky enough to get you to your goals. Younger age = more risk because of a longer timeline. Closer to retirement means you should take less risk.
- You will need to check in at least once every year to consider rebalancing. Checking in two or three times is probably fine.

Put the advice in this chapter to work and get out of your own way. Don't make it any more complicated than it needs to be. If you absolutely must get paid financial advice, then you should use a fee-only financial advisor under a fiduciary contract that utilizes a flat-fee model and has extensive experience with physicians.

Chapter 12:
How Much Do I Need?

"If you've won the game, stop playing!"
~ William J. Bernstein, MD PhD

We have discussed the dynamics of making a plan to keep our debt low, pay down our student loans, and even invest our money. To what end, though? What is our target? When will we stop? That's what this chapter is about. We will discuss the financial independence retire early (FIRE) movement, how much you need for retirement, and safe withdrawal rates. This will likely serve as a primer, because it would be impossible to write a chapter on creating a drawdown plan for retirement. That would require an entirely different book.

Financial Independence Retire Early (FIRE)

The FIRE movement started with a book called "Your Money or Your Life" by Vicki Robin. I am not sure this was her intention when she wrote it in 1992, but the spark from her book ignited a FIRE movement which is now propelled by a group of people who recognize two key concepts. First, in order to retire early you need to save enough money to be able to fund the lifestyle you want, which means building wealth by destroying debt and aggressively investing. This may sound familiar to you after reading this book. Second, these people noticed that if they decreased their spending on lifestyle (read: frugal), they didn't need as much money as they previously thought in order to retire. And if you combined these two concepts (building wealth quickly and living frugally), many people in the FIRE community have proven that it's possible to reach FIRE quickly.

The reason I mention these two concepts in this chapter is because the second concept is paramount to answering the question "how much do I need to retire?" Well, as with anything, it depends. In this case it mostly depends on your anticipated lifestyle in retirement. If you plan on living on $50,000 per year, then you probably only need $1.25-$1.5 million dollars. If you want to retire on $150,000 annually, you will need much more.

The second concept (frugality) is inextricably linked to the first (a high savings rate). Achieving a high savings rate ($\geq$30%) is impossible without limiting your spending. This book—and hopefully prior experiences—has taught you better. Your goal should be to live a debt-free life as early as possible. For this reason, the amount of money you are spending in retirement should be predicated on the idea that you are 100% debt free. No mortgage, car loans, student loans, or consumer debt. If you elect, your kids' college educations will also be funded through a 529, scholarships, part-time jobs, or by some other means.

For this reason, please remember that your retirement needs will likely be limited to a few specific things: taxes, food, utilities, health care, charitable giving, and travel/leisure. That's it. When you are talking about those six categories, $10,000 per month sounds like a ton of money, right? The lower the monthly retirement allowance, the earlier financial independence will become a reality. I've always contended that a financially independent physician is a better doctor. So is a doctor who has a clear plan for achieving it.

Note: It is outside the scope of this book, but if you do retire early recognize that you cannot access your 401K/403B until age 59.5 or else you'll be subject to a 10% penalty, which will deplete your account rather rapidly. You will need to rely on other means in your earlier years such as a taxable account, Roth ladder conversion, or a cash money pile. I have written about bridging this gap in retirement on my website for anyone who is interested in reading further.

How Much Do I Need?

The traditional answer to this question assumes that you plan to retire at age 60 or 65. If that is the case, then all you need to do is to figure out your annual expenses as outlined above and multiply that number by 25 (also known as "The 25 X Rule"). Odds are, you won't live past 90. And even if you do, a good portfolio will continue to outpace inflation. For example, if you need $100,000 a year in retirement (remember, no debt!), you will need $2.5 million dollars to retire. That's your number to retire at age 60-65. These numbers come from the Trinity Study, which is outlined below. Before we move on, I should note that your number may grow with each passing year. As inflation occurs, your annual spending may increase with it. Therefore, the number you need to retire at a retirement age is 25 times your current annual spending.

If you want to retire early, you need to be a little more conservative. Say you want to be able to retire at age

50 or 55. You need to take your annual number and multiply it by 30 or 35. So, again using the $100,000 annual number, you would need $3.0-3.5 million dollars to retire. This makes sense, because obviously more money is going to be required over a longer period of time if we want to retire earlier. If, however, you could be content on retiring on $8,000 per month, then you would only need $2.4-2.8 million dollars. You can get to that number pretty quickly if you are investing aggressively. For example, if you are saving $75,000 per year and earning 6% annually, you will arrive at this number in 19 or 20 years. If you finished training at age 35, that's age 55. Look at you, you early retiree. If your investments earn an 8% return, you'll get there a little sooner—17 years, or age 51.5 years old.

You'll notice that the numbers above do not include social security or pensions. I am not sure how much we can count on those forms of retirement income, particularly for those of us who are 15-30 years away from collecting on it. I wouldn't bet my future retirement on money that is not guaranteed. Get to your number on your own and the rest will just be gravy.

Safe Withdrawal Rate

A safe withdrawal rate (SWR) is the percentage of money you can take from your retirement nest egg and be reasonably assured that the money will last for your entire retirement. There are many opinions on the SWR during retirement (usually ranging from 3-6%). For example, if you have $3 million saved up for retirement and use a 3% SWR, you can take out $90,000 (3% of $3 million) each year.

That said, most discussions on SWR start with the Trinity Study, which looked at multiple 30-year timelines for retirement and the chance that you would still have money left based on various stock/bond asset allocations at the end of the 30 years. The chart is below in Figure 1. You'll notice asset allocations on the left and various time frames for each allocation. On the top are the various withdrawal rates. Where these two numbers intersect is the percentage of people who had money left in their account at the end of that specific time frame.

Portfolio Composition/ Payout Period	Withdrawal Rate as a % of Initial Portfolio Value									
	3	4	5	6	7	8	9	10	11	12
100% Stocks										
15 Years	100	100	100	91	79	70	63	55	43	34
20 Years	100	100	88	75	63	53	43	33	29	24
25 Years	100	100	87	70	59	46	35	30	26	20
30 Years	100	95	85	68	59	41	34	34	27	15
75% Stocks-25% Bonds										
15 Years	100	100	100	95	82	68	64	46	36	27
20 Years	100	100	90	75	61	51	37	27	20	12
25 Years	100	100	85	65	50	37	30	22	7	2
30 Years	100	98	83	68	49	34	22	7	2	0
50% Stocks-50% Bonds										
15 Years	100	100	100	93	79	64	50	32	23	13
20 Years	100	100	90	75	55	33	22	10	0	0
25 Years	100	100	80	57	37	20	7	0	0	0
30 Years	100	95	76	51	17	5	0	0	0	0
25% Stocks-75% Bonds										
15 Years	100	100	100	89	70	50	32	18	13	7
20 Years	100	100	82	47	31	16	8	4	0	0
25 Years	100	93	48	24	15	4	2	0	0	0
30 Years	100	71	27	20	5	0	0	0	0	0
100% Bonds										
15 Years	100	100	100	71	39	21	18	16	14	9
20 Years	100	90	47	20	14	12	10	2	0	0
25 Years	100	46	17	15	11	2	0	0	0	0
30 Years	80	20	17	12	0	0	0	0	0	0

Figure 1. Safe Withdrawal Rate findings from Trinity Study[24]

---

[24] : Bogleheads Safe Withdrawals Rate
https://www.bogleheads.org/wiki/Safe_withdrawal_rates .
Accessed January 26th, 2019.

176

There are a few important points to take away from the Trinity Study findings. First of all, you need to keep investing in some percentage of stocks in order to keep up with inflation and not deplete your portfolio. Notice that even at a 3% withdrawal rate, only 80% of people had money left after 30 years if they invested in 100% bonds. Every other category made it because they continued to take some risk. Second, if you invested in 75% stocks/25% bonds you had a 98% chance to make it to the end of the 30 years with money left at a 4% withdrawal rate.

Many people say that the SWR is 4% annually. I mention this for your education, but please take this as a guide and not a strict rule. If you retire early, it is wise to be a little more conservative initially at 3%-3.5%. If your portfolio crushes it for the first ten years of your retirement, you can probably stand to take out more than 4%. That said, you can also protect against some issues by saving a little more than you actually need, which is why I encourage those interested in early retirement to aim for 30 X their anticipated annual income instead of just 25 X.

Regardless, a 4% SWR is a good place to start this conversation and will help make sense of the numbers mentioned above for retirement. In the example above for traditional retirement, we said that if someone wanted $100,000 annually and retired at age 60 or 65 they would need ($100,000 x 25) = $2.5 million dollars. If you take 4% of this $2.5 million dollars, guess what you get? $100,000. The math is reciprocal.

There are a few caveats that should be mentioned regarding the SWR:

1. Just because money remained at the end for people in this study doesn't mean there was a lot. That could mean many sleepless nights at the end hoping the money lasts, which is not where you want to be. Dying poor is not the goal. Solutions to this include using a smaller SWR, or saving more than you need.
2. There is something called a sequence of returns risk (SORR), which is the risk that the market might decline dramatically right after someone retires. People who haven't saved enough (or haven't prepared other pots of money to use during such a time) might be at risk to lose a substantial sum of their retirement savings if they are drawing down during that time. The best way to get past this problem is to have a pot of cash saved for one to two years' worth of retirement expenses available in a low-risk vehicle that will hopefully keep up with inflation (CDs, money market account, etc.). Alternatively, you could save a little more than you need or draw down a little less than you planned.
3. It is worth mentioning twice: The 4% SWR is more of a guide than a rule. You may have to be flexible in retirement in down years, particularly if they occur early on in retirement.

One note of caution

I have mentioned Dr. William Bernstein before. He is the retired neurologist who became a financial advisor. In his book called "The Investor's Manifesto: Preparing for Prosperity, Armageddon, and Everything in Between" he has the following to say about what encompasses a SWR:

"When all is said and done, I still know of no better risk analysis tool for retirees under the age of 70 then this simple narrative: At a 2 percent withdrawal rate, your nest egg will survive all but catastrophic institutional and military collapse; at 3 percent, you are probably safe; at 4 percent, you are taking real chances; and at 5 percent and beyond, you should consider annuitizing most, if not all, of your nest egg."

For the record, I am not a fan of annuities. The point Dr. Bernstein is trying to drive home is that 3-4% is really the SWR in his mind. Above that, you start taking more and more risk. A withdrawal rate at or above 5% should concern you greatly.

Take Home:

"If you've won the game, stop playing."

- Plan to accumulate 25-30 X your annual retirement expenditures as "your number" for retirement. This is based on the Trinity Study.
- It is necessary to take risk in order to get market returns that will achieve your financial goals. Once you get to financial independence, you need to start assuming less risk.
- Note: I didn't say that you should abandon risks all together. We saw what happened to those people in the Trinity study above who transitioned to 100% bonds. It didn't work out so well.
- How much of your portfolio you should convert to bonds, TIPS, or annuities (if any) is

debatable and people have varying opinions on this topic.

It is still good advice to stop playing the game once you have won. Don't take more risk than you need once you have won the game. It's perfectly fine to continue to work part time (or full time) to save up more than you need, but don't keep taking unmitigated risks in the market. I preach being conservative. You probably need 25X your current annual income in order to consider retirement. You need 30-35 for an early retirement. A SWR will be around 3-3.5%. The point remains that you should get to your number and maybe a little beyond and then transition to a safer portfolio.

Chapter 13:
Asset Protection

"Dream as if you'll live forever.
Live as if you'll die today."
~ James Dean

In medieval times, castles were built with some very important protective barriers. Sometimes this consisted of a wall that was difficult to scale. Other times, a moat and a drawbridge were included. Maybe the castle also included archery towers to shoot down would-be attackers.

Your personal finances should be as fortified and protected as those castles. Instead of a wall or moat to protect your castle, you will require asset protection. A lot of hard work goes into earning your education and training. This places doctors in a prime position for earning capital during your lifetime. Without protection, all of this work can be lost in a single catastrophic illness or event. This chapter discusses the nuts and bolts of protecting your assets.

Be a Good Doctor

The best asset protection you can afford is to be good at your job. Some might think the reason that I mention this first is because of the medical-legal world in which we currently work. If so, they would only be half right. Medical-legal protection is important and the best way to do this is to be good at your job and the "three Cs" (competent, compassionate, and a complete documenter). However, this is not the only reason to be good at your job. Being good at your job may help you move up through the academic ranks or become partner in private practice. It may provide opportunities to make more money or land a job that you thought was out of reach. And, of course, being a good doctor means you are taking good care of patients—the ultimate goal.

So, if you are a medical student or resident reading this book, please do study. Read for 30 minutes a day, no matter how tired you are. If you miss a day, make it up on the weekends. Knowledge can conquer a lot of fear. The best wealth-building device you have in training is to be well trained. Don't put the cart before the horse on this one.

Life Insurance

This was touched on in chapter 3 where we discussed conflicts of interest, but it bears repeating. Do not buy permanent life insurance, which can go by many names including whole life insurance, cash value insurance, or universal life insurance. Let me repeat that. You should *not* mix investing and insurance. That's definitely part of the 20% you need to know to get 80% of the results. Insurance salespeople get paid a high commission (50-110% of your first year's annual premium) to sell you this product, which is why they do a good job selling it. They make it sound like permanent life insurance is the best thing since sliced bread and rattle off the ten reasons it is perfect for you. Please, do your research.

Remember the story above about the golf coach at the interview who had to make cold calls to friends and family to prove he could sell a product that he knew nothing about? The truth is that insurance agents who tout whole life insurance are trained in sales, not investing. Permanent life insurance is not a good investment vehicles and the death benefit is much more expensive to pay for than a term life insurance product. Of course, the insurance salesman will tell you that it is "not an insurance vehicle" at all. That won't stop them, though, from making it sound like an investment the entire time that they pitch it to you.

The other option (there is really only one) is term life insurance. How should you buy it? You should buy it from an independent insurance agent that can get you quotes from several different companies. An independent insurance agent Is one who is not tied to a specific insurance company that only allows the agent to sell their product.

Fortunately, life insurance is pretty black and white. You are either dead or alive. Getting approved for this benefit—as dark as it may seem—is pretty straightforward, assuming that you do not have some devastating personal or family medical history. You probably do not need term life insurance unless you are married or have children. I know more than one physician who was sold a life insurance policy when they simply didn't need it.

Here are some guidelines for life insurance:
- Use an independent insurance agent that has experience working with physicians. Being

independent allows an agent to get you multiple quotes.

- Buy insurance from a reputable company so that you can count on it being there if you should need to collect on this benefit. A company that goes under isn't going to do you much good when your family needs it.
- Buy enough coverage. This stuff is not expensive. During residency, $750,000 of coverage for both my wife and me cost us $50 per month.
- Buy it as soon as you have reason to need a death benefit (spouse/children). Every day that passes you risk getting diagnosed with an illness that could prevent you from qualifying. So, buy it sooner rather than later.
- Get as much as you can afford for the same reason listed in the bullet point above (health changes as you age). I took $750,000 during residency and then substantially increased mine after training. I am not going to disclose the amount here as I have no need for you to convince my wife to hire an assassin!
- If you are reading this book, then you might consider getting an annually renewable policy where the rate is dirt cheap the first several years (as in during residency) and then ratchets up thereafter when you can afford it.
- At some point, you'll become financially independent and will no longer be able to justify the premium as you self-insure.

Disability Insurance

Disability insurance (DI) is not as clean cut as life insurance because the definition of "disability" is many shades of grey. Therefore, you need to make sure that you get the right stuff. However, before we get to that, let's discuss the first question:

When should I get disability insurance?

This is a really important question that I didn't know the answer to in medical school and it may cost my family and me greatly someday. Remember the story from the conflicts of interest chapter about when I applied for disability insurance as a fourth-year medical student? A classmate of mine in medical school had a brother who worked for a reputable insurance company. He was looking for now clients, and since I just had my first kid I was ripe for the opportunity to get life insurance. So, I gave him a call. At this point, I was only a fourth-year medical student. We sat down and I told him I wanted life insurance. He asked if I was healthy. To which I replied that I was otherwise healthy aside from an essential tremor (diagnosed by a neurology resident as I aptly, but shakily, performed my first lumbar puncture in my third year of medical school). He told me to apply for DI despite the fact that (I would find out later) I was going into one of the hardest specialties to insure, anesthesiology. I said no three times before he talked me into it. I suppose this is why they have to learn to make those cold calls in interviews.

Well, long story short my application was flat out denied. No rider for my tremor was offered. The result was a straight denial. The reason that this is important is that many hospitals with residency and fellowship programs offer "guaranteed" DI policies that forego medical underwriting so that they never look into your medical history. Literally the only stipulation for these policies is that you cannot have been denied for DI previously. That's it. Thanks to my friend's brother, I do not have personal disability insurance to this day and must rely on the group policy provided by my employer.

So, to answer the question, "when should you get disability insurance?"

1. If you are without medical problems and have had recent lab work at your PCP, then you can consider applying as soon as you have an income worth protecting (i.e., residency).
2. If you have known medical problems or laboratory abnormalities, then WAIT to get the guaranteed policy offered in training. Once you have that policy in hand, you can feel free to apply wherever you want. You will not lose the guaranteed policy once it's yours, even if you are later denied by another insurance company. However, you cannot go the opposite direction with this like I did.

Where should I buy DI?

The answer here is the same as it was for life insurance. Doctors looking for DI need to find an independent agent that has experience working with physicians. You can find recommended insurance agents on The Physician Philosopher website. Apply to multiple reputable companies to get estimates based on your medical history. Take the best policy at the cheapest price. Remember, disability policies provide a lot more shades of grey than do life insurance policies. What exactly defines "disabled?" Paying for a more expensive policy with better own-occupation, specialty-specific disability language is worth it (compared to a cheaper policy with language that won't help you when you need it).

Since disability insurance can be so grey, it is critical to use an independent agent. Agents that are tied to a specific company cannot offer you the same experience, because they have a conflict of interest to sell the products to which they are bound. The DI insurance agent needs to have experience working with doctors because the definition of "own-occupation" coverage is incredibly important. Certain companies have changed their "own-occupation" language in a way that may not reflect a physician's needs. Some of the same companies that have done this also do not allow independent agents to sell their products. For this reason, get someone who has experience selling disability products to physicians and who can get you a contract from the best-fit company.

What features are key for DI?

This is not an exhaustive list, but here are some of the key aspects of a DI policy:

- Try to secure DI before finishing training so that you can more appropriately "stack" a group policy on top of your personal DI policy. Remember, if you have pre-existing medical conditions, get the guaranteed policy first!
- Your goal should be to replace 100% of your post-tax (take home) income.
- Apply to multiple companies to get the best pricing (use an independent agent).

- Be wary of replacing a policy in hand with a new policy (there is a conflict of interest for insurance salespeople to get a new commission). Do your research first.
- Purchasing a cost-of-living adjustment (COLA) rider, which increases your DI payment with inflation, is an option. If you cannot afford this AND get maximum DI insurance, I would max out the DI insurance instead of getting the COLA rider.
- Get the future purchase option that allows you to buy more insurance—without additional medical underwriting—when your income goes up following training. If you are out of training when you first apply, just get the most you can.
- You want a non-cancellable and guaranteed policy. Any insurance agent offering you something different does not deserve your business.

Other Insurances

There are other insurance products that you need, but they are fortunately much more straightforward. For example, insure your car and house. That's pretty easy, right? Take the highest deductible you can to lower the premiums.

You should also get umbrella insurance. The stuff is ridiculously cheap. Get a few million dollars to protect you from things not covered by your auto or home insurance. For example, say your kid slides off an icy road in their car and hits a bystander. Whatever expenses are not covered by your auto policy would slide into your umbrella insurance policy. It will also cover you when your kids' friend breaks a femur trying to jump off an exercise trampoline into the pool from the second floor deck—but misses the pool and lands on the concrete. It's cheap, but important, insurance.

One of the more important insurances you can buy is "self-insurance." You have a high income, and should have enough money around for three to six months of expenses, or for an emergency. Therefore, you do not need insurance for your phone, computer, or new TV. If it breaks, you can afford to replace it. The insurance companies do the math to make sure that they make out ahead most of the time. Don't give them the pleasure of getting the better end of the deal unless you have to. Along the same lines, take the highest deductible for your insurance products. You are hedging your bets that you won't use it, because you can afford it even if it does become necessary.

Side Hustles

Speaking of self-insurance, one of the better ways you can protect your main income is by having multiple income streams. Ideally, this would be passive income that you get whether you work or not. But any side income will help you get to your goals faster. As long as you enjoy it—and it doesn't burn you or your relationships out—then I recommend pursuing it.

Examples of side income include making a medical invention, writing a book, locum tenens work outside your main gig, blogging, expert witness work, coaching, and real estate. Find your passion outside of work. It may provide additional income for retirement or protect you from turbulent times.

Think about that last sentence. We previously discussed a safe withdrawal rate of around 4%. For every $1,000,000 you have in your retirement accounts, you can anticipate that providing $40,000 each year (4% of $1,000,000). So, if you have a side hustle with a consistent income of $40,000 per year; guess what? You now need $1,000,000 less in your retirement accounts before you are financially independent. Of course, this assumes that you continue this side income stream into retirement, but the point is that side hustles can be awesome.

Dealing With a Bear Market

This may seem like a strange place for me to include dealing with a down market, but it is certainly a way to protect your assets. After all, if you make a great plan, dollar-cost average your money into the market (i.e. put money in with each paycheck over a long time period), and then sell it all at the lowest price because the market is too painful to bear … well, that would be one of the greatest financial mistakes you can make. Do not buy high and sell low. Slaying the bear market is a key aspect of asset protection.

The key to protecting your assets can be summed up in four words: ***Stick to the plan!***

Here are four ways to do just that:
1. Perfect behavioral finance. Recognize that a bear market WILL happen during your lifetime. Probably more than once. The risk of the market that allows your stocks to surge in one market is the same risk that will make them

plummet. It is simply part of the game. Recognize that and then stop looking at your portfolio!

2. A bear market means that stock prices are down. Rather than looking at your $1,000,000 portfolio turning into $750,000 and doing the worst imaginable thing (selling), look at it another way! When prices go down, you have the opportunity to buy stocks "on sale." When they come back up, you will have purchased them at a discount.

3. If the above fails, pay that fee-only advisor acting as a fiduciary for an hour's worth of advice on why you should not sell your portfolio in a down market. However, I just gave you all of that information for the cost of this book. Maybe I should have sold the book for $200?

Bear markets are not black swans. They are not exceptions. And they certainly are not bad luck. What they are is *expected*. When you are young in your career—if you are wise—you should hope for a long, hard decade of a down market. When it recovers, you will be getting paid handsomely. When you are in the golden ages of your investing career, you should have purchased a high enough percentage of bonds to deal with the turbulence.

Take Home

Don't throw your hard work away! For those that like checklists and timelines, the following might be helpful as a summary:

- Life insurance: Purchase when you have someone who stands to lose greatly when you die (spouse/kids).
  - In residency/fellowship purchase enough to pay off all of your debts and provide for a year or two of income. Typically, this will range $500,000 - $1,000,000.
  - Attending physicians should increase total coverage to the amount you would consider to be financially independent. Bare minimum, cover all of your debts and any anticipated future expenses (weddings, college, etc.). This number is probably $2-5 million total.
- Disability insurance: Pursue this as soon as you have an income to protect (i.e., in residency). Buy it the day before you get disabled. If you don't know when that'll be, then by it as soon as possible. [If you have pre-existing conditions, get the guaranteed policy that waives the medical exam prior to applying for a non-guaranteed policy].
- The obvious stuff: If you have a house or car, insure them.
- Umbrella insurance: This stuff is dirt cheap. Buy it once you can afford to max out your house and car insurance, which is usually required to get umbrella insurance. The typical range is $2-3 million worth of coverage.
- Self-insure when possible. This is the purpose of an emergency fund.
- Side hustles can protect your income stream.
- Stick to the plan and be a good doctor!

Remember how challenging it was to get into medical school, to get through residency training, and to save your hard-earned money? Don't watch all of that hard work go to waste by failing to protect your assets. While some of this may be common sense to you, it always surprises me how many people fail to take care of this aspect of personal finance. Don't be that person. Be smart and check these necessary boxes off so that you can sleep at night.

Chapter 14:
The Balance

"The purpose of life is not to be happy. It is to be useful, to be honorable, to be compassionate, to have it make some difference that you have lived and lived well."
~ Ralph Waldo Emerson

My wife used to be a server when she was in high school and college. Her favorite customers were the elderly people who would walk in, sit down, and promptly order dessert first. After this happened a few times, my wife gathered up the courage to ask one of the couples why. They responded, *"Honey, when you are our age, you never know which meal might be your last. So, you might as well start with the best part."* I think the same could have been said for this chapter. Maybe we should have started here, but here we are saving one of the most important –and savory— chapters for last.

Balancing Now and Then

Remember those candies called "Now and Laters"? I always thought that was an interesting name. You can either have something now or you can have it later, right? Isn't that why we make fun of people who want to "have their cake and eat it, too"?

The point is that you can have something now or you can save it for later. In no area is this truer than in personal finance. We actively delay putting money into our bank accounts to spend it. Instead, we invest it with

195

the anticipation that we will need it at some later date. In essence, we are paying our future self now by deferring money we could be enjoying today.

While this book has spent ample time teaching you how to do that, I do want you to take something else away, too. It is possible to take frugality, saving, and a drive to achieve financial independence too far. If you delay your gratification completely, you might be miserable. Don't get to the point where you are working through misery so that one day you can enjoy the good life. Please, don't do this. Learn to live a little even now. Enjoy life. Take vacations. Spend time with your family and friends.

In this vein, I want to talk about a few specific items to help us keep the right perspective. I say "us" because I need to hear this just as much as any of you reading this book.

First, the commodity we are really trying to accrue is time; not money. Money is a means to an end. It is not the end itself. For this reason, don't view time off as money lost. This is particularly hard for people in shift work specialties. Take time off so that you don't burn out.

Second, it is an admirable and worthwhile goal to learn how to be content with little. New cars, homes, and clothes will not make you happier. If you can learn to be content with little, it will be very easy to be content with more. However, if you are miserable now; odds are you will be miserable later. Spending money will not solve this problem. The secret is in learning the skill of contentment, which will serve you well no matter how wealthy you become later in life.

Third, learn to balance the here and now with your future goals. Use the 10% rule (or an adaptation of it) to live a little now while setting yourself up for success later. I guess in this sense, you can actually have some of your cake now and eat the rest later, too. Spend a little bit of money to enjoy life, and then be frugal with the rest so that you can build wealth. Let others laugh at you when you don't drive a doctor's car or live in a doctor's house for the first few years out of training. You'll be laughing all the way to the bank when you are financially independent in your mid-40s or early 50s. They'll ask how you did it and you can show them a picture of those things they gave you a hard time about at the beginning of your career.

Use Financial Independence to Combat Burnout

The subtitle says it all. Recognize that financial independence (FI) is a weapon to be wielded. You do not have to wait until you are completely independent to get out of a job you hate. Instead, you can go part time earlier in your career and create a glide path to retirement. Many have found this not only makes them happier, but often makes them more productive when they are at work. Oftentimes, burned out doctors find relief in part time work.

If you are now working 1 FTE, consider cutting back to 0.7 FTE. Having an extra day or two off of work each week will likely make a world's difference in terms of happiness. Also, this will show you that people can, in fact, live on less, which will perfect another important lesson on the frugality side of the FIRE argument. Remember, half of the answer to financial success is your saving rate, and the other half is learning to live on less.

Instead of cutting back days at work, you could also consider using your FI to leverage focusing more on the aspects of the jobs you love. Maybe you enjoy doing research. Cutting back may allow you more time to focus on that. Or maybe it's a side hustle you've become passionate about. It could also be a certain aspect of your job that you don't like such as performing a certain procedure that you simply don't enjoy. The point here is that financial independence provides choices and flexibility.

Design an Intentional Life

This book is all about providing information so that you can make intentional decisions with your life. If you are ever at a fork in the road that requires financial planning decisions, I want to share a helpful way to think through these problems.

George Kinder, philosopher-turned-public accountant, came up with three questions to help people plan their finances.[25] Given the target audience of this book, hopefully you'll appreciate the perspective from which these questions arise. Here they are, directly from Mr. Kinder:

---

[25] Get Rich Slowly. https://www.getrichslowly.org/george-kinder-three-questions-about-life-planning/ Accessed January 25th, 2019.

1) "I want you to imagine that you are financially secure, that you have enough money to take care of your needs, now and in the future. The question is, how would you live your life? What would you do with the money? Would you change anything? Let yourself go. Don't hold back your dreams. Describe a life that is complete, that is richly yours."

2) "This time, you visit your doctor who tells you that you have five to ten years left to live. The good part is that you won't ever feel sick. The bad news is that you will have no notice of the moment of your death. What will you do in the time you have remaining to live? Will you change your life, and how will you do it?"

3) "This time, your doctor shocks you with the news that you have only one day left to live. Notice what feelings arise as you confront your very real mortality. Ask yourself: What dreams will be left unfulfilled? What do I wish I had finished or had been? What do I wish I had done? What did I miss?"

It is extremely useful to go through the three Kinder questions. Sit down. Write out the answers with a loved one. Then, design your life and your finances in such a way that your goals will be reached. After all, having loads of money without living your life well is quite pointless.

Take Home

The take home is simple.
- Minimize debt.

- Live the same lifestyle after you finish training for 2-3 years so that you can use a substantial amount of your earning capital to build wealth by paying down debt and investing aggressively.
- Save 25-30% of your income towards retirement, keep your lifestyle in a reasonable place, and enjoy early financial independence.
- Be sure to live a balanced lifestyle along that way. Allow yourself to enjoy a little bit of the here and now while you build a firm foundation for your future self in retirement.

Above all, remember that money is a tool to build the life you want to live. Money itself is not the goal. At this point I hope you will agree that personal finance is not so complicated that you cannot do it yourself. However, if you ever need help, you also now know where to find it: a non-conflicted source of financial advice.

Subscribe and review

If you ever need my help, you can reach out to me by subscribing to The Physician Philosopher website (https://thephysicianphilosopher.com/subscribe). And, if you found this book helpful, then consider leaving a review on Amazon so that others can find it, too!